BTEC Level 2 First Study Skills Guide in Health and Social Care

Welcome to your Study Skills Guide! You can make it your own – start by adding your personal and course details below...

Learner's name: _____

BTEC course title: _____

Date started: _____

Mandatory units:

_____

_____

_____

Optional units:

_____

_____

_____

_____

Centre name: _____

Centre address:

_____

_____

_____

Tutor's name: _____

Published by Pearson Education Limited, a company incorporated in England and Wales, having its registered office at Edinburgh Gate, Harlow, Essex, CM20 2JE. Registered company number: 872828

Edexcel is a registered trademark of Edexcel Limited

Text © Pearson Education Limited 2010

First published 2010

13 12 11
10 9 8 7 6 5 4 3

British Library Cataloguing in Publication Data
A catalogue record for this book is available from the British Library

ISBN 978 1 84690 574 2

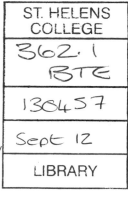
Typeset and edited by Sparks Publishing Services Ltd
Cover design by Visual Philosophy, created by eMC Design
Cover photo/illustration © Getty Images; Stuart Redler
Printed in Malaysia, KHL-CTP

Acknowledgements
The author and publisher would like to thank the following individuals and organisations for permission to reproduce photographs:

Alamy Images: Jurgen Eis / imagebroker 71, Ace Stock Limited 55, Jacky Chapman, Janine Wiedel Photolibrary 11, Janine Wiedel Photolibrary 36; **South Downs College:** 74; **Corbis:** 60, Comstock 5; **iStockphoto:** Eliza Snow 40; **Pearson Education Ltd:** Steve Shott 23, Ian Wedgewood 33; **TopFoto:** John Powell 19

Cover images: *Front:* **Getty Images:** Stuart Redler

All other images © Pearson Education

Every effort has been made to contact copyright holders of material reproduced in this book. Any omissions will be rectified in subsequent printings if notice is given to the publishers.

Websites
Go to www.pearsonhotlinks.co.uk to gain access to the relevant website links and information on how they can aid your studies. When you access the site, search for either the title BTEC Level 2 First in Health and Social Care or the ISBN 9781846905742.

Disclaimer
This material has been published on behalf of Edexcel and offers high-quality support for the delivery of Edexcel qualifications.
This does not mean that the material is essential to achieve any Edexcel qualification, nor does it mean that it is the only suitable material available to support any Edexcel qualification. Edexcel material will not be used verbatim in setting any Edexcel examination or assessment. Any resource lists produced by Edexcel shall include this and other appropriate resources. Copies of official specifications for all Edexcel qualifications may be found on the Edexcel website: www.edexcel.com

Contents

Popular progression pathways

General qualification	Vocationally related qualification	Applied qualification
Undergraduate Degree	BTEC Higher National	Foundation Degree
GCE AS and A level	BTEC National	Advanced Diploma
GCSE	BTEC First	Higher (L2) and Foundation (L1) Diplomas

Your BTEC First course
Early days

Every year many new learners start BTEC Level 2 First courses, enjoy the challenge and successfully achieve their award. Some do this the easy way; others make it harder for themselves.

Everyone will have different feelings when they start their course.

Case study: Thinking positively

Sharmeen is preparing to begin her BTEC First in Health and Social Care.

'When I applied for a place on the BTEC course back in January, it all seemed really exciting and sounded fascinating. I really liked the idea of learning about this vocational area, through units related specifically to health and social care. The assignments the tutor described sounded really interesting and I couldn't wait to get started!

Now the course is about to begin and my nerves are starting to set in. I've never had any experience in health and social care, whereas other people I know who have done the course in the past had done it at GCSE already, or maybe they did their Year 10 work experience in a health and social care setting, such as a pre-school. I remember feeling like this when I first went to secondary school and within a few weeks I wondered what I had got so worked up about. But this is different, isn't it?

My tutor at school says that lots of people feel this way before they start a new course or school/college, job or any part of their life, and that whenever you have a negative thought, you should try to find a way to make it positive.'

Here are some examples:

Negative thought – 'The other people on the course will all be cleverer than me.'

Positive thought – 'This is a great opportunity to learn from others, as well as the tutors. There might be some students who are better at using their initiative than me, but there are bound to be things I can do that others aren't so good at.'

Negative thought –'I don't think I like old people.'

Positive thought – 'Vocational experience is all about trying things and finding out whether you like them or not. If you don't, after the vocational experience, you don't have to do it again!'

About your course

What do you know already?

If someone asks you about your course, could you give a short, accurate description? If you can, you have a good understanding of what your course is about. This has several benefits.

Four benefits of understanding your course
1 You will be better prepared and organised.
2 You can make links between the course and the world around you.
3 You can check how your personal interests and hobbies relate to the course.
4 You will be alert to information that relates to topics you are studying, whether it's from conversations with family and friends, watching television or at a part-time job.

Read any information you have been given by your centre. You can also check the Edexcel website for further details – go to www.edexcel.com.

Interest/hobby	How this relates to my studies

What else do you need to know?

Five facts you should find out about your course

1. The type of BTEC qualification you are studying.
2. How many credits your qualification is worth.
3. The number of mandatory units you will study and what they cover.
4. How many credits the mandatory units are worth.
5. The number of optional units you need to study in total and the options available in your centre.

Case study: What will I study?

Sophie is preparing to begin her BTEC First in Health and Social Care.

'When I first started thinking about doing a course in health and social care, I thought it would be a case of going to the nearest centre and saying, "I would like to do health and social care please!" But when my tutor said there were different courses in health and social care and I should look into all of the centres and courses in my area, I realised there is a much larger range than I originally thought.

I had to think carefully about which course would be best for me. I had done my Year 10 work experience at a nursing home and really enjoyed working with service users who had dementia and so I was thinking of becoming a mental health nurse. My tutor pointed out that I might need particular subjects, such as psychology and biology, if I wanted to be a nurse and so I looked into the health and social care courses that covered these subjects in their units. I was also disappointed with my GCSE results last year, although I did do well in English. Based on all of this, I decided to take a one-year course which will help me progress to a BTEC National

in Health and Social Care next year.

My cousin Logan is just entering Year 10 and is studying the BTEC First Extended Certificate in Health and Social Care. His course is different to mine, as he is studying fewer units. His course is also taught over two years and he is doing some GCSEs alongside it. He is also considering doing a BTEC National Diploma in the future, but he is keeping his options open as he also enjoys history and he cannot decide between humanities and his interest in health and social care.'

The course Logan is taking has fewer credits than Sophie's. He is also studying for a longer period of time which means that he will have less time for his course on his timetable each week and more time to study other subjects, such as his GCSEs. Other than Sophie's BTEC, the only other course she is taking is a GCSE maths resit.

Even though they are both studying BTEC First in Health and Social Care, Sophie's course contains more units than Logan's. They both have some units in common, but Sophie's course has different optional units to Logan's.

BTEC FACT

BTEC First Certificate = 15 credits

BTEC First Extended Certificate = 30 credits

BTEC First Diploma = 60 credits

Generally, the more credits there are, the longer it takes to study for the qualification.

TRY THIS

Find out which optional units your centre offers. To check the topics covered in each unit go to www.edexcel.com.

TOP TIPS

If you have a choice of optional units in your centre and are struggling to decide, talk through your ideas with your tutor.

Activity: How well do you know your course?

Complete this activity to check that you know the main facts. Compare your answers with a friend. You should have similar answers except where you make personal choices, such as about optional units. Your tutor can help you complete number 9.

1 The correct title of the BTEC award I am studying is:

2 The length of time it will take me to complete my award is:

3 The number of mandatory units I have to study is:

4 The titles of my mandatory units, and their credit values, are:

5 The main topics I will learn in each mandatory unit include:

Mandatory unit	Main topics

6 The number of credits I need to achieve by studying optional units is:

7 The titles of my optional units, and their credit values, are:

8 The main topics I will learn in each optional unit include:

Optional unit	Main topics

9 Other important aspects of my course are:

10 After I have achieved my BTEC First, my options include:

Introduction to the health and social care sector

Choosing to study a BTEC First in Health and Social Care is an excellent decision to make for lots of different reasons. The health and social care sector employs a huge number of people who undertake a wide range of jobs using an array of different skills and techniques.

Doing a health and social care course is more than just learning about how to be a nurse. There are so many different jobs in a range of settings that you might not even have heard of them! Studying a BTEC First in Health and Social Care gives you an opportunity to explore the different avenues that you could pursue in the future.

Think of the last time you went to the doctor or to hospital. Like most people, you would have been focused on the main people who treated you, such as the doctor or nurse. You probably didn't stop to consider the many other people without whose contribution the health and social care system would not be able to function as effectively as it does. Becoming part of the health and social care sector means that you have to work as part of a team. This is very important, as it would be impossible for one health and social care professional to look after one patient from the start of their care to the very end.

BTEC FACTS

Did you know that the UK's National Health Service (NHS) is one of the biggest employers in the world?

Your BTEC course will help you develop all-round skills, like communication.

Case study: A step in the right direction

Ali completed his BTEC First in Health and Social Care in 2003. He has since gone on to work for a funeral director as an embalmer preserving bodies from the time of death until they can be buried or cremated.

'Ever since I was little, I knew that I wanted to help and look after people when they were ill. I did originally think about becoming a nurse, as that was the only job role that I had heard of and knew about.

I became interested in working with the deceased after going on my first work placement at a nursing home. While I was there, an elderly resident died in her sleep. The woman's family asked me if I wanted to go to her funeral as she and I had become close. I had never been to a funeral before and had no idea what to expect. What I found very interesting, was the comfort that the funeral director brought to the family. I had never thought about the support the rest of the family would need when someone is ill or has died. I had always thought that working in health and social care would be just about helping the patients themselves.

For my next placement, I went to a funeral director and thoroughly enjoyed it. It was there that I saw my first dead body and met the embalmer who preserves the bodies until the time of burial or cremation. This spurred me to go to my local college and enrol on a BTEC National Diploma in Health and Social Care. I then applied to funeral directors in my local area and was employed by one as an assistant while studying once a week to become an embalmer.

I would never have considered this pathway if it hadn't been for my BTEC First in Health and Social Care.'

Skills you need for your sector

It is essential that anyone working in a health and social care setting has certain skills in order to make sure they are capable of doing their job and that everyone does things in the same way as others. This is important, as everyone working in the same way, and with the right skills, will ensure that health and social care environments can all work together to improve the health and well-being of service users.

The wide variety of jobs within the health and social care sector all require different skills. For example, a hospital porter must be fit and have stamina as much of this work involves helping to transport patients and moving furniture around the workplace. A receptionist's stamina on the other hand isn't as important, but they do need good organisational skills to be efficient in their work.

However, there are some skills required by many of the jobs in health and social care:

- Communication skills

    These are very important for working in health and social care as most jobs involve communicating with other people, whether they are colleagues, service users or other members of the public. Nobody likes a stroppy receptionist or a rude doctor!

- Teamwork skills

    These are also needed because it is impossible for one person to look after a patient's entire care and treatment. Health and social care professionals often work as part of a multi-disciplinary team working together to treat a patient.

Activity: Working with other people

Read the case study and answer the questions below.

Jade is a very keen rugby player. During a bad tackle in a match, Jade dislocated her knee and tore some ligaments. An ambulance was called and Jade was put on a stretcher and taken to hospital. Once at the hospital, Jade was seen in A&E and given an x-ray.

It was decided that Jade needed surgery and so she was later anaesthetised and underwent an operation. After the operation, Jade was taken to a ward where she spent the night recovering from the surgery. The next day, after breakfast and taking her medicine, Jade was taught how to use crutches and to move about.

When Jade returned home, she went to physiotherapy to regain full movement in her knee. After six months of treatment, Jade returned to rugby.

Make a list of all the health professionals who worked together to help Jade get back to playing rugby.

Could they have done it if they hadn't worked as a team? Why (not)?

There are some skills that will be developed by all learners on the BTEC First in Health and Social Care.

- Understanding the sector

  You will gain an understanding of how the health and social care sector works, by investigating organisations and job roles from various areas of the sector.

- Understanding the different routes into health and social care

  By looking into the different areas and pathways you can take in health and social care, such as a career in health care or in social care, the course will help you to explore the avenues you take next, such as progressing to a BTEC National in Health and Social Care and going to university, or maybe moving straight into the world of work.

Regardless of the pathway you are studying, there are some essential personal, learning and thinking skills (PLTS) you will develop while you are completing your BTEC course. See page 81 for more information on these.

More about BTEC Level 2 Firsts

What is different about a BTEC Level 2 First?

How you learn

Expect to be 'hands-on'. BTEC Level 2 Firsts are practical and focus on the skills and knowledge needed in the workplace. You will learn new things and learn how to apply your knowledge.

BTEC First learners are expected to take responsibility for their own learning and be keen and well-organised. You should enjoy having more freedom, while knowing you can still ask for help or support if you need it.

How you are assessed

Many BTEC First courses are completed in one year, but if you are taking GCSEs as well, you may be doing it over two years or more. You will be assessed by completing **assignments** written by your tutors. These are based on **learning outcomes** set by Edexcel. Each assignment will have a deadline.

TOP TIPS

You can use your Study Skills Guide with the Edexcel Student Book for BTEC Level 2 First Health and Social Care (Edexcel 2010). It includes the main knowledge you will need with tips from Edexcel experts, Edexcel assignment tips, assessment activities and up-to-date case studies from industry experts, plus handy references to your Study Skills Guide.

TOP TIPS

Doing your best in assignments involves several skills, including managing your time so that you don't get behind. See pages 22 and 23 for tips on managing your time more efficiently.

BTEC FACTS

On a BTEC course you achieve individual criteria at pass, merit or distinction for your assignments. You will receive a pass, merit or distinction **grade** for completed units and then one of these three grades for the whole course.

Case study: Reasons for choosing a BTEC First in Health and Social Care

Anais looks back at the assignments she completed when studying the BTEC First in Health and Social Care.

'I chose this course because I knew it was all assignment based and that suits me as I really don't like exams. Before I started the course, I thought the assignments were going to be like doing GCSE coursework, but in fact it is different. I prefer doing the assignments on the BTEC course as they are more structured and easier to follow.

Each assignment has separate tasks rather than one big essay and they ask you to do completely different things. For example, one task asks you to create a leaflet on healthy eating, while the next asks you to work in groups and create a role-play scenario of someone experiencing discrimination! These tasks are focused towards particular criteria enabling you to achieve a pass, merit or distinction grade.

What I found very surprising was that one task would be to get a pass and the next task would be for a merit, so you knew exactly which criteria you were aiming for. When you're doing GCSE coursework, one task covers all the grades and you may be unaware what you've got to do to get an A* compared to a C.

My class was also given an assignment planner with the submission dates for all the assignments. This was really useful as it helped me plan and manage my time efficiently. There were a few assignments where I didn't do as well as I would have liked to and so my tutor allowed me to resubmit them. The feedback from the tutor told me where I had gone wrong and what I needed to do to improve. I used this guidance to redo and add to the tasks. He also gave me new deadlines to work to and these fitted in around my other assignments.'

Getting the most from your BTEC

Getting the most from your BTEC involves several skills, such as using your time effectively and working well with other people. Knowing yourself is also important.

Knowing yourself

How would you describe yourself? Make some notes here.

If you described yourself to someone else, would you be able to sum up your temperament and personality, identify your strengths and weaknesses and list your skills? If not, is it because you've never thought about it or because you honestly don't have a clue?

Learning about yourself is often called self-analysis. You may have already done personality tests or careers profiles. If not, there are many available online. However, the information you gain from these profiles is useless unless you can apply it to what you are doing.

Your personality

Everyone is different. For example, some people:

- like to plan in advance; others prefer to be spontaneous
- love being part of a group; others prefer one or two close friends
- enjoy being the life and soul of the party; others prefer to sit quietly and feel uncomfortable at large social gatherings
- are imaginative and creative; others prefer to deal only with facts
- think carefully about all their options before making a decision; others follow their 'gut instincts' and often let their heart rule their head.

Case study: Personality types

Many people think that anyone involved in health and social care will have a very kind and caring personality; the kind of person who always wants to talk and help solve other people's problems. Where some of these personality traits might be useful to someone wanting to work in health and social care, they are not the only qualities needed to succeed in a BTEC First in Health and Social Care.

Take Manoss and Saffron. Both are studying on a BTEC First in Health and Social Care course, but they have very different personalities.

Manoss loves to be in the spotlight and enjoys the practical elements of the course. He excels on his work placements and really wants to pursue a career as an ambulance technician, but he has to work harder when completing written work. He can also be a bit bossy when completing group tasks and tends to go with his gut instinct when coming up with new ideas rather than trying several out.

Saffron, on the other hand, hates being the centre of attention. She is well organised and conscientious, vital skills for someone working in the administrative side of health and social care. She is creative and likes solving problems, which means she does particularly well in assignments which involve considering a number of different options and finding the most suitable for the dilemma at hand. Saffron is, however, not as assertive as she could be, particularly when working as part of a team. She sometimes takes a back seat when decisions are made and is not forceful enough when it comes to getting the group to consider her own ideas.

TRY THIS

Imagine one of your friends is describing your best features. What would they say?

Personalities in the workplace

There's a mix of personalities in most workplaces. Some people prefer to work behind the scenes, such as many IT practitioners, who like to concentrate on tasks they enjoy doing. Others love high-profile jobs, where they may often be involved in high-pressure situations, such as paramedics and television presenters. Most people fall somewhere between these two extremes.

In any job there will be some aspects that are more appealing and interesting than others. If you have a part-time job you will already know this. The same thing applies to any course you take!

Your personality and your BTEC First course

Understanding your personality means you can identify which parts of your course you are likely to find easy and which more difficult. Working out the aspects you need to develop should be positive. You can also think about how your strengths and weaknesses may affect other people.

- Natural planners find it easier to schedule work for assignments.
- Extroverts like giving presentations and working with others but may overwhelm quieter team members.
- Introverts often prefer to work alone and may be excellent at researching information.

BTEC FACT

All BTEC First courses enable you to develop your personal, learning and thinking skills (**PLTS**), which will help you to meet new challenges more easily. (See page 81.)

Activity: What is your personality type?

1a) Identify your own personality type, either by referring to a personality test you have done recently or by going online and doing a reliable test. Go to page 90 to find out how to access an online test.

Print a summary of the completed test or write a brief description of the results for future reference.

b) Use this information to identify the tasks and personal characteristics that you find easy or difficult.

	Easy	Difficult
Being punctual		
Planning how to do a job		
Working neatly and accurately		
Being well organised		
Having good ideas		
Taking on new challenges		
Being observant		
Working with details		
Being patient		
Coping with criticism		
Dealing with customers		
Making decisions		
Keeping calm under stress		
Using your own initiative		

	Easy	Difficult
Researching facts carefully and accurately		
Solving problems		
Meeting deadlines		
Finding and correcting own errors		
Clearing up after yourself		
Helping other people		
Working as a member of a team		
Being sensitive to the needs of others		
Respecting other people's opinions		
Being tactful and discreet		
Being even-tempered		

2 Which thing from your 'difficult' list do you think you should work on improving first? Start by identifying the benefits you will gain. Then decide how to achieve your goal.

Your knowledge and skills

You already have a great deal of knowledge, as well as practical and personal skills gained at school, at home and at work (if you have a part-time job). Now you need to assess these to identify your strengths and weaknesses.

To do this accurately, try to identify evidence for your knowledge and skills. Obvious examples are:

- previous qualifications
- school reports
- occasions when you have demonstrated particular skills, such as communicating with customers or colleagues in a part-time job.

Part-time jobs give you knowledge and skills in a real work setting.

TOP TIPS

The more you understand your own personality, the easier it is to build on your strengths and compensate for your weaknesses.

Activity: Check your skills

1 Score yourself from 1 to 5 for each of the skills in the table below.

1 = I'm very good at this skill.

2 = I'm good but could improve this skill.

3 = This skill is only average and I know that I need to improve it.

4 = I'm weak at this skill and must work hard to improve it.

5 = I've never had the chance to develop this skill.

Enter the score in the column headed 'Score A' and add today's date.

2 Look back at the units and topics you will be studying for your course – you entered them into the chart on page 9. Use this to identify any additional skills that you know are important for your course and add them to the table. Then score yourself for these skills, too.

3 Identify the main skills you will need in order to be successful in your chosen career, and highlight them in the table.

Go back and score yourself against each skill after three, six and nine months. That way you can monitor your progress and check where you need to take action to develop the most important skills you will need.

English and communication skills	Score A (today) Date:	Score B (after three months) Date:	Score C (after six months) Date:	Score D (after nine months) Date:
Reading and understanding different types of texts and information				
Speaking to other people face to face				
Speaking clearly on the telephone				
Listening carefully				
Writing clearly and concisely				
Presenting information in a logical order				
Summarising information				
Using correct punctuation and spelling				
Joining in a group discussion				
Expressing your own ideas and opinions appropriately				
Persuading other people to do something				
Making an oral presentation and presenting ideas clearly				
ICT skills	Score A (today) Date:	Score B (after three months) Date:	Score C (after six months) Date:	Score D (after nine months) Date:
Using ICT equipment correctly and safely				
Using a range of software				
Accurate keyboarding				
Proofreading				
Using the Internet to find and select appropriate information				
Using ICT equipment to communicate and exchange information				
Producing professional documents which include tables and graphics				
Creating and interpreting spreadsheets				
Using PowerPoint				

Maths and numeracy skills	Score A (today) Date:	Score B (after three months) Date:	Score C (after six months) Date:	Score D (after nine months) Date:
Carrying out calculations (e.g. money, time, measurements, etc) in a work-related situation				
Estimating amounts				
Understanding and interpreting data in tables, graphs, diagrams and charts				
Comparing prices and identifying best value for money				
Solving routine and non-routine work-related numerical problems				

Case study: Previous skills and experience

Some people join a BTEC First in Health and Social Care because they have already had some experience of caring; others simply because they have an interest in the subject.

Amy started caring for her mother at the age of eight, when her mother was diagnosed with a condition that left her wheelchair-bound and suffering from the illness on a regular basis. Amy and her mother had no other family to help, so Amy quickly learnt to be self-sufficient as the main carer for her mother, helping her to dress, eat and do everyday household chores.

Amy is classed as a 'young carer' and she enjoys caring for her mother. Amy decided that she would like to pursue a career in caring, therefore making the BTEC First in Health and Social Care an obvious choice for her when it came to her Year 10 options.

Yasmin, on the other hand, had no formal experience of caring when she joined the same course. She did, however, gain an interest in working with children when her school ran a 'virtual babies' project. Each learner had to look after a virtual baby as if they were real, by

feeding, changing nappies, burping the baby etc. Yasmin was found to be the best in the class at caring for her baby. Yasmin also loves watching hospital dramas and enjoys seeing the gruesome injuries suffered by some patients and the operations they undergo.

Both girls brought very different skills to the course. Amy already had a good grasp of the health and social care sector, understanding the different job roles and support available to those in need. She was able to contribute effectively in class discussions and use her experience and knowledge as examples in her assignments.

Yasmin brought a great deal of imagination and creativity to the course. She was quick to pick up different terminology and health and social care phrases and she was very good at relating the theories to different real life settings. Her baby skills also stood her in good stead for the units on Individual Needs in Health and Social Care and Human Lifespan and Development.

Have you got any previous experience that will help you to complete the units you are studying?

Managing your time

Some people are brilliant at managing their time. They do everything they need to and have time left over for activities they enjoy. Other people complain that they don't know where the time goes.

Which are you? If you need help to manage your time – and most people do – you will find help here.

Why time management is important

- It means you stay in control, get less stressed and don't skip important tasks.
- Some weeks will be peaceful, others will be hectic.
- The amount of homework and assignments you have to do will vary.
- As deadlines approach, time always seems to go faster.
- Some work will need to be done quickly, maybe for the next lesson; other tasks may need to be done over several days or weeks. This needs careful planning.
- You may have several assignments or tasks to complete in a short space of time.
- You want to have a social life.

Avoiding time–wasting

We can all plan to do work, and then find our plans go wrong. There may be several reasons for this. How many of the following do *you* do?

Top time-wasting activities
1 Allowing (or encouraging) people to interrupt you.
2 Not having the information, handouts or textbook you need because you've lost them or lent them to someone else.
3 Chatting to people, making calls or sending texts when you should be working.
4 Getting distracted because you simply must keep checking out MySpace, Facebook or emails.
5 Putting off jobs until they are a total nightmare, then panicking.
6 Daydreaming.
7 Making a mess of something so you have to start all over again.

Planning and getting organised

The first step in managing your time is to plan ahead and be well organised. Some people are naturally good at this. They think ahead, write down their commitments in a diary or planner, and store their notes and handouts neatly and carefully so they can find them quickly.

How good are your working habits?

Improving your planning and organisational skills

1 Use a diary or planner to schedule working times into your weekdays and weekends.

2 Have a place for everything and everything in its place.

3 Be strict with yourself when you start work. If you aren't really in the mood, set a shorter time limit and give yourself a reward when the time is up.

4 Keep a diary in which you write down exactly what work you have to do.

5 Divide up long or complex tasks into manageable chunks and put each 'chunk' in your diary with a deadline of its own.

6 Write a 'to do' list if you have several different tasks. Tick them off as you go.

7 Always allow more time than you think you need for a task.

Talking to friends can take up a lot of time.

TRY THIS

Analyse your average day.

How many hours do you spend sleeping, eating, travelling, attending school or college, working and taking part in leisure activities?

How much time is left for homework and assignments?

TOP TIPS

If you become distracted by social networking sites or email when you're working, set yourself a time limit of 10 minutes or so to indulge yourself.

BTEC FACT

If you have serious problems that are interfering with your ability to work or to concentrate, talk to your tutor. There are many ways in which BTEC learners who have personal difficulties can be supported to help them continue with their studies.

Case study: Getting yourself organised

Harrison reflects on his organisational skills.

'My mum always said if I can put anything off until tomorrow, I will. She has a point. When I started my BTEC First in Health and Social Care, we were told that being organised and staying on top of the work were really important. After that talk I had good intentions to do the work as it came.

When we started work on our first big assignment, my tutor explained that we should complete the tasks after every session, while what we had done was still fresh in our minds. For the first few weeks I did. But then I started to leave it until later so I could watch television or just hang around with my mates. Then I would promise myself that I'd catch up with it tomorrow or later in the week.

Before I knew it I was several sessions behind with the tasks. With the deadline approaching, I had to go over my rough notes and try to think back to what we'd done in each session. I ended up in a right panic and it took ages, much longer than it would have done if I'd just got on with it as my tutor had suggested.

After that I decided to turn over a new leaf and for the second assignment my goal was to complete my work as soon as I got home, no matter what. I got into the routine of coming home, grabbing a drink from the fridge, sitting down and getting on with it. It worked well because, when it came to handing it in, all I had to do was just check it through. The bonus was that I ended up getting better grades.'

Do you ever put things off until another day and end up rushing at the last minute?

Find a time in your day to complete any homework tasks and stick to it. Make it part of your daily routine.

Activity: Managing time

1 The correct term for something you do in preference to starting a particular task is a 'displacement activity'. In the workplace this includes things like often going to the water cooler to get a drink, and constantly checking emails and so on online. People who work from home may tidy up, watch television or even cook a meal to put off starting a job.

Write down *your* top three displacement activities.

2 Today is Wednesday. Sajid has several jobs to do tonight and has started well by making a 'to do' list. He's worried that he won't get through all the things on his list and because he works on Thursday and Friday evenings that the rest will have to wait until Saturday.

   a) Look through Sajid's list and decide which jobs are top priority and *must* be done tonight and which can be left until Saturday if he runs out of time.

   b) Sajid is finding that his job is starting to interfere with his ability to do his assignments. What solutions can you suggest to help him?

Jobs to do

- File handouts from today's classes

- Phone Tom (left early today) to tell him the time of our presentation tomorrow has been changed to 11 am

- Research information online for next Tuesday's lesson

- Complete table from rough notes in class today

- Rewrite section of leaflet to talk about at tutorial tomorrow

- Write out class's ideas for the charity of the year, ready for course representatives meeting tomorrow lunchtime

- Redo handout Tom and I are giving out at presentation

- Plan how best to schedule assignment received today – deadline 3 weeks

- Download booklet from website ready for next Monday's class

---

 **TRY THIS**

Write down your current commitments and how long they take each week. Then decide those that are top priority and those that you could postpone in a very busy week.

Getting the most from work experience

On some BTEC First courses, all learners have to do a **work placement**. On others, they are recommended but not essential, or are required only for some optional units. If you are doing one, you need to prepare for it so that you get the most out of it. The checklists in this section will help.

Before you go checklist

1. Find out about the organisation by researching online.

2. Check that you have all the information you'll need about the placement.

3. Check the route you will need to take and how long it will take you. Always allow longer on the first day.

4. Check with your tutor what clothes are suitable and make sure you look the part.

5. Check that you know any rules or guidelines you must follow.

6. Check that you know what to do if you have a serious problem during the placement, such as being too ill to go to work.

7. Talk to your tutor if you have any special personal concerns.

8. Read the unit(s) that relate to your placement carefully. Highlight points you need to remember or refer to regularly.

9. Read the assessment criteria that relate to the unit(s) and use these to make a list of the information and evidence you'll need to obtain.

10. Your tutor will give you an official log book or diary – or just use a notebook. Make notes each evening while things are fresh in your mind, and keep them safely.

While you're on work placement

Ideally, on your first day you'll be told about the company and what you'll be expected to do. You may even be allocated to one particular member of staff who will be your 'mentor'. However, not all firms operate like this and if everyone is very busy, your **induction** may be rushed. If so, stay positive and watch other people to see what they're doing. Then offer to help where you can.

TRY THIS

You're on work experience. The placement is interesting and related to the job you want to do. However, you've been watching people most of the time and want to get more involved. Identify three jobs you think you could offer to do.

While you're there

1. Arrive with a positive attitude, knowing that you are going to do your best and get the most out of your time there.

2. Although you may be nervous at first, don't let that stop you from smiling at people, saying 'hello' and telling them your name.

3. Arrive punctually – or even early – every day. If you're delayed for any reason, phone and explain. Then get there as soon as you can.

4. If you take your mobile phone, switch it off when you arrive.

5. If you have nothing to do, offer to help someone who is busy or ask if you can watch someone who is doing a job that interests you.

6. Always remember to thank people who give you information, show you something or agree that you can observe them.

7. If you're asked to do something and don't understand what to do, ask for it to be repeated. If it's complicated, write it down.

8. If a task is difficult, start it and then check back that you are doing it correctly before you go any further.

9. Obey all company rules, such as regulations and procedures relating to health and safety and using machinery, the use of IT equipment and access to confidential information.

10. Don't rush off as fast as you can at the end of the day. Check first with your mentor or supervisor whether you can leave.

Coping with problems

Problems are rare but can happen. The most common ones are being bored because you're not given any work to do or upset because you feel someone is treating you unfairly. Normally, the best first step is to talk to your mentor at work or your supervisor. However, if you're very worried or upset, you may prefer to get in touch with your tutor instead – do it promptly.

TOP TIPS

Observing people who are skilled at what they do helps you learn a lot, and may even be part of your **assignment brief.**

Getting experience of work in the health and social care sector

You may be studying a course where completing some vocational experience is essential to achieving the qualification. There are some health and social care courses that don't require vocational experience in order to achieve the overall qualification and you should check with your tutor whether you are required to do a work placement or not.

Getting work placements in health and social care can be difficult for students as age can be a barrier. Many 'interesting' placements may be off limits as the law can often stipulate that you must be over a particular age before you can embark on them. Even if you are allowed to go on the placement, sometimes all you can do is observe the service providers carrying out their daily tasks, rather than get 'hands on'.

Most placements will also require you to have a Criminal Records Bureau check (often known as a CRB check) carried out before you start to make sure you are suitable to work with vulnerable people. If you have ever had any police warnings, cautions or convictions for any matter, however serious, you should discuss this with your tutor and with the work placement team before you embark on your vocational experience.

There are, however, many good health and social care placements, as well as other ways of gaining additional experience of working in the health and social care sector while studying for your BTEC First in Health and Social Care. Before you start planning your placement, you need to be aware of the wide range of settings within the health and social care sector.

List as many health, social and childcare settings you can think of.

Health	Social	Childcare
hospital	residential home	nursery

Look at your list and highlight any settings which you are interested in. Would the settings you have selected be likely to accept you for work experience? What reasons might they give for not accepting learners?

Pick one setting for the three categories below and list five job roles you might find in that setting.

Health	Social	Childcare
(e.g. hospital)	(e.g. residential home)	(e.g. nursery)
1	1	1
2	2	2
3	3	3
4	4	4
5	5	5

Highlight any jobs in your table which you would be interested in observing.

Investigate where these settings are in your local area. You could use a local map and phone book, or the internet to help your research. Write down the addresses and phone numbers below.

Contact the settings to arrange a placement.

Activity: Volunteering

When looking to become a volunteer, you need to consider how often you would be expected to do so. This would depend entirely on what you are volunteering for. Some volunteer roles ask for specific times and days, others are a little more general. Some places are happy for new volunteers to offer their availability and then they find them tasks to do.

If you decide to become a volunteer, you may be assisting in running or organising activities and fundraisers, or you may be working one to one with service users. This is good practice for job or further education interviews you may have to undertake in the future, as it shows that you have been keen and willing to help in society and learn and develop your skills.

Being a volunteer is a regular commitment and you will need to prove yourself as a reliable member of the team. People will be relying on you to provide a service and to give 100% towards that service. You will often have to prove that you are trustworthy before being allocated more major roles.

There are plenty of health and social care organisations where you could volunteer and so gain valuable experience within a health and social care setting, for example St John Ambulance. Create a list or table of organisations, with some information about what they do, where you could possibly work as a volunteer.

Case study: Gaining experience in the sector

Lai is in Year 11 and completing her second year of a BTEC First in Health and Social Care. When she joined the course, Lai was already a student counsellor for the younger year groups at her school and had been since Year 9.

'It was joining the student counselling team in Year 9 that actually got me interested in doing the BTEC. I joined when I was 14 and absolutely loved it. We hold sessions at lunchtime twice a week where anyone (including staff!) can come and share their problems with individual counsellors. We mostly have individuals from the younger year groups telling us they are worried about homework and falling out with friends, but occasionally we have some individuals from the older year groups in too as they trust us to maintain confidentiality and not judge them.

I think the work I do with the student counselling has helped me do well on my BTEC course. I get lots of experience of working with individuals on a one-to-one basis

and I have really learned to appreciate how important good communication skills are. It has really increased my confidence, as it is up to me to try to help the individuals who have come to seek advice. On the BTEC course, when we are having class discussions, it is easier to understand and remember the main themes and topics, as I can relate them to the vocational experience I have gained.

I also had a vocational experience work placement in Year 10 which my school organised for all students, regardless of the course they were studying. My placement was at a centre for children with learning disabilities. Even though being a school counsellor was not the same as the role I was performing on the placement, I felt more comfortable than I thought I would, as I found myself communicating effectively with the children. I think this was a result of my previous vocational experiences and lessons.'

Working with other people

Everyone finds it easy to work with people they like and far harder with those they don't. On your course you'll often be expected to work as a team to do a task. This gives you practice in working with different people.

You will be expected to:

- contribute to the task
- listen to other people's views
- adapt to other people's ways of working
- take responsibility for your own contribution
- agree the best way to resolve any problems.

These are quite complex skills. It helps if you understand the benefits to be gained by working cooperatively with other people and know the best way to achieve this.

BTEC FACT

An important part of your BTEC course is learning how to work positively and productively with other people.

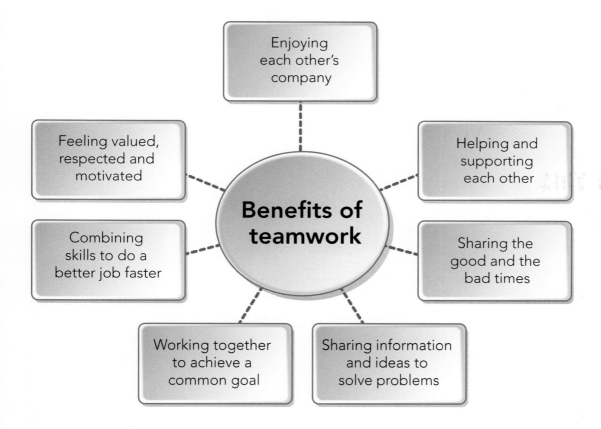

The benefits of good working relationships and teamwork

Golden rules for everyone (including the team leader!)

The secret of a successful team is that everyone works together. The role of the team leader is to make this as easy as possible by listening to people's views and coordinating everyone's efforts. A team leader is not there to give orders.

Positive teamwork checklist

✔ Be loyal to your team, including the team leader.

✔ Be reliable and dependable at all times.

✔ Be polite. Remember to say 'please' and 'thank you'.

✔ Think before you speak.

✔ Treat everyone the same.

✔ Make allowances for individual personalities. Give people 'space' if they need it, but be ready to offer support if they ask for it.

✔ Admit mistakes and apologise if you've done something wrong – learn from it but don't dwell on it.

✔ Give praise when it's due, give help when you can and thank people who help you.

✔ Keep confidences, and any promises that you make.

Do you:

a) shrug and say nothing in case he gets upset

b) ask why he didn't text you to give you warning

c) say that it's the last time you'll ever go anywhere with him and walk off?

Which do you think would be the most effective – and why?

Case study: Teamwork in health and social care

Joe remembers a group task that didn't go according to plan.

'Our task was to produce a creative and therapeutic activity and demonstrate it to a different class in their tutorial. It was quite a nervewracking task, as it required us to plan the activity, gather the resources ourselves and present it to a class which wasn't our own, to learners who we didn't really know. What we did think was good at the time, was that we could choose our own group members to work with.

My friends and I all instantly chose to go with each other, thinking we would be the best group. However, very quickly things started to go wrong. One person in our group tried to take over and wouldn't really listen to anyone else's ideas. Another group member kept forgetting our arranged meetings and so we would have to plan things without her. Another

member just didn't do any work as he thought we would do it all for him.

When it came to the day of the activity, I remember feeling really unorganised and unprepared. One group member didn't show up with the resources we needed. Luckily for us our tutor had some spare resources we could borrow. The activity went all right in the end, but our group really needed to work together better and think of each other more.

Afterwards, our tutor asked us to reflect on the activity and say what we felt went well or badly and what we could do in the future to improve this. It was interesting what the other team members said, as they felt I hadn't been very approachable! I have to say I did think the group task was going to be a piece of cake, but I misjudged how hard it can be to work effectively in a team.'

There are many benefits to be gained from working as a team.

Activity: Teamwork

Groupwork is central to learning on a BTEC First in Health and Social Care. You will find that you will be asked to work in groups for many of your lessons, whether it is just to discuss a topic, carry out some research or produce a presentation to perform in front of the rest of your class. Therefore it is vital that the group work as a team to ensure the time is used productively.

Taking part in a presentation is hard work. There will be times when you are actively involved in the process and times when you will need to sit quietly while someone else in your group presents. It is vital that your concentration and focus are maintained throughout. Behaviour, such as chatting to others or texting, can be distracting to those involved and those watching the presentation. It suggests you find the content of the presentation boring and so why should others listen and be interested?

Come up with three golden rules for good behaviour while your group is presenting.

1
2
3

Practising a presentation is very important and it is often the time for taking risks and trying things out. It is therefore essential that there is a supportive atmosphere in the room. Group members must feel comfortable with each other and they must feel they can try out ideas without being laughed at or ridiculed.

Come up with three golden rules for supporting other members of the group during practice sessions.

1
2
3

It is vital that each team member carefully prepares for each practice, with preparation which might involve:

- learning your subject so you don't have to read from a sheet of paper
- creating cue cards to help
- making a PowerPoint presentation or other resource to show during the presentation.

Undertaking required preparation is important for your own progress, as well as the grades you are awarded on the course. It is also important for the group, as failure to undertake required tasks may impact on the overall quality of the presentation work produced.

Come up with three golden rules for preparing for practice.

1
2
3

Teamwork during presentation practice

When carrying out any group task, one of the most important skills is communication. Good communication skills ensure that messages are clear and the task at hand progresses as it should. When taking part in group discussions, meetings and tasks, it is important that you express yourself clearly while also taking into consideration the views and feelings of others.

Learners from the BTEC First Diploma in Health and Social Care were in a group meeting discussing a number of different ideas for their 'job shop' promotion for Unit 10 Health and Social Care Services. When looking at the design ideas for a display put forward by one learner, another member of the group said, 'This idea is rubbish. It will never work'.

What might the effect of this comment be on:
a) the learner whose ideas were being discussed?

b) other learners in the group?

When you think an idea is not right for a project it is important that you say so. You must however try and provide constructive feedback rather than just saying that something is no good!

For example, another way of communicating concern over the idea might have been to say:

'You've obviously worked hard on the design, but I'm not sure how it will work in practice as it seems very complicated.'

Why might this response have been more appropriate? Consider the statements below and suggest a more appropriate comment in each case.

What was said...	How it might have been said...
'This is just the same as the last idea you came up with. You haven't even tried.'	
'My ideas for the job shop are way better than yours.'	
'Why can't you be quiet and let someone else speak?'	
'This is the first time you've been here in weeks. I don't see why we should have to listen to you.'	

Getting the most from special events

BTEC First courses usually include several practical activities and special events. These enable you to find out information, develop your skills and knowledge in new situations and enjoy new experiences. They may include visits to external venues, visits from specialist speakers, and team events.

You may get the chance to visit a hospital and speak to a nurse about their typical working day.

Most learners enjoy the chance to do something different. You'll probably look forward to some events more than others. If you're ready to get actively involved, you'll usually gain the most benefit. It also helps to make a few preparations!

Case study: A visit to a specialist museum

Petrina and the other students on the BTEC First in Health and Social Care at Hampshire College visited a museum that specialises in anatomy and physiology.

'I'd been to different museums on previous trips when I was at school and always found them really boring, so when I found out we were going to a museum as part of my course, I assumed I had seen it all before. I didn't even know what the museum contained. I just thought it would be another boring trip to go on.

What I didn't realise, was that the trip was to a museum containing loads of different, but real, human body parts. Our tutor had arranged for us to have a guided tour around the museum, so you didn't get bored reading all the little pieces under the displays on your own. The tour guide told us about each display and included some really funny stories about the human body too.

I enjoyed the tour of the museum, particularly the bit where we got to see some x-rays of people's broken bones and funny objects they had swallowed! My favourite part of the trip was when we were allowed to have a hands-on study of different bones and teeth and we were able to use the microscopes to see bone development and structure.

Overall the visit was a real surprise. It's really spurred me on to do well on the course as I definitely want to work as a medical technician or in a laboratory in the future.'

Special events checklist

✔ Check you understand how the event relates to your course.

✔ If a visit or trip is not something you would normally find very interesting, try to keep an open mind. You might get a surprise!

✔ Find out what you're expected to do, and any rules or guidelines you must follow, including about your clothes or appearance.

✔ Always allow enough time to arrive five minutes early, and make sure you're never late.

✔ On an external visit, make notes on what you see and hear. This is essential if you have to write about it afterwards, use your information to answer questions in an assignment or do something practical.

✔ If an external speaker is going to talk to your class, prepare a list of questions in advance. Nominate someone to thank the speaker afterwards. If you want to record the talk, it's polite to ask first.

✔ For a team event, you may be involved in planning and helping to allocate different team roles. You'll be expected to participate positively in any discussions, to talk for some (but not all) of the time, and perhaps to volunteer for some jobs yourself.

✔ Write up any notes you make as soon as you can – while you can still understand what you wrote!

Observing professional health and social care work

Many BTEC Firsts in Health and Social Care learners undertake visits and excursions as part of their course. Often visits will include trips to hospitals, residential homes, museums and other health and social care settings.

Before a visit, it is a good idea to find out about the work you are going to see and to do some research into the setting you are going to visit. This can often be done by looking at the relevant setting's website. What do you think would be useful to find out? Add your answers to the spidergram below.

> **What would be useful to find out before going on a visit to a health and social care setting?**

TRY THIS →

At the last minute, you're asked to propose a vote of thanks to a visiting speaker on behalf of your class. What would you say?

Resources and research

Understanding resources

Resources are items that help you do something. The most obvious one is money! To obtain your BTEC First award, however, your resources are rather different.

Different kinds of resources

Physical resources

Physical resources are things like textbooks, computers and any specialist equipment.

- Popular textbooks, laptops for home use and specialist equipment may need to be booked. Leaving it until the last minute is risky.
- You can ask for help if you don't know how to use resources properly.
- You should check what stationery and equipment you need at the start of your course and make sure you have it.
- You need to look after your resources carefully. This saves money and time spent replacing lost items.

People as resources

There are many people who can help you through your course:

- family members who help and support you
- your tutor
- friends in your group who collect handouts for you and phone you to keep you up-to-date when you're absent
- librarians and computer technicians, at your centre or your local library
- expert practitioners.

Expert practitioners

Expert practitioners have worked hard to be successful in their chosen area. They know the skills and knowledge needed to do the job properly. They can be invaluable when you're researching information (see page 43). You can also learn a lot by watching them at work, especially if you can ask them questions about what they do, what they find hard and any difficulties they've had.

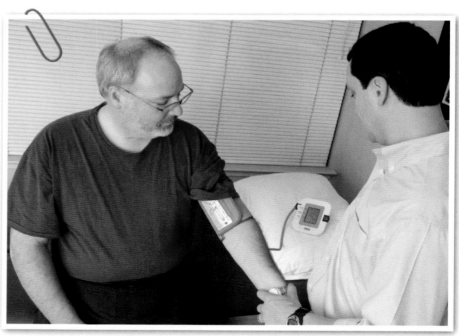

A health care worker measures and records a man's blood pressure.

Try to observe more than one expert practitioner:

- It gives you a better picture about what they do.
- No single job will cover all aspects of work that might apply to your studies.
- You may find some experts more approachable and easy to understand than others. For example, if someone is impatient because they're busy it may be difficult to ask them questions, or if someone works very quickly you may find it hard to follow what they're doing.

If you have problems, just note what you've learned and compare it with your other observations. And there's always the chance that you're observing someone who's not very good at their job! You'll only know this for certain if you've seen what people should be doing.

Create your own resource list

When studying on a BTEC First in Health and Social Care you will need to use a range of physical resources and equipment to complete the projects and assignments,

- Library-based resources

  Books, magazines and journals will be a valuable resource when undertaking research. Whether you are researching equal opportunities legislation in order to show how to overcome discrimination, or finding out about the job role of a podiatrist in the NHS, books, magazines and journals will be essential.

- Internet resources

  Websites can be a valuable source of information when researching the work of practitioners. Websites based on careers can be very helpful when researching particular job roles and NHS websites show the performance of hospitals in local areas, as well as showing what they specialise in. The main NHS website also contains a self-help guide along with an encyclopaedia and updates on health concerns and other health matters.

- Stationery

  Much of the work you undertake on a BTEC First in Health and Social Care will be produced in some written format. It may be in the form of a poster, leaflet or an essay, so you should make sure you are equipped with pens and pencils, as well as a file in which to keep handouts, notes and work you complete for homework tasks. A small notebook might also be useful for making notes when undertaking visits or on work experience.

- Other equipment

  Some units may require you to have access to specific equipment and while most of this will be provided by your centre, some items of personal use will not. For example, if you are gaining vocational experience in a health and social care setting, you will need to have appropriate clothing for your work placement. This could range from wearing a polo shirt in a nursery to wearing scrubs in a hospital.

Use the grid below to create your own resource list.

Your tutor may suggest items to include which are relevant to the units you are studying. You could also visit your centre's library to gather information about the relevant books you may need to refer to on your course.

Library resources (books, magazines)

Internet resources (websites)

Stationery

Equipment (clothing)

Finding the information you need

The information explosion

There are lots of different ways to find out information – books, newspapers, magazines, TV, radio, CDs, DVDs, the internet. And you can exchange information with other people by texting, sending an email or phoning someone.

All this makes it much easier to obtain information. If you know what you're doing, you can probably find most of what you need sitting at a computer. But there are some dangers:

- Finding exactly what you want online takes skill. You need to know what you're doing.
- It's easy to get too much information and become overwhelmed.
- It's unlikely that everything you need will be available online.
- The information you read may be out of date.
- The information may be neither reliable nor true.

Define what you are trying to find. (The more precise you are, the more likely you are to find what you're looking for.) → Know where to look for it. (Remember: the internet is not the only source of information.) → Recognise when you have found appropriate information.

Know what to do with information once you've found it. (Make sure that you understand it, interpret it correctly and record the source where you found it.) ← Know when to stop looking (especially if you have a deadline).

Finding and using information effectively

Before you start

There are four things that will help you look in the right place and target your search properly.

Ask yourself ...	Because ...	Example
Exactly what do I need to find out?	It will save you time and effort.	If you need information about accidents, you need to know what type of accident and over what time period.
Why do I need this information and who is going to read it?	This puts the task into context. You need to identify the best type of information to obtain and how to get it.	If you're making a poster or leaflet for children, you'll need simple information that can be presented in a graphical format. If, however, you're giving a workplace presentation on accidents, you'll need tables and graphs to illustrate your talk.
Where can I find it?	You need to consider whether your source is trustworthy and up to date. The internet is great, but you must check that the sites you use are reliable.	To find out about accidents in the workplace you could talk to the health and safety at work officer. To find examples of accidents in your local area you could look through back copies of your local newspaper in the local library or newspaper offices.
What is my deadline?	You know how long you have to find the information and use it.	

Your three main sources of information are:
- libraries or learning resource centres
- the internet
- asking other people, for example through interviews and questionnaires.

Researching in libraries

You can use the learning resource centre in your school or college, or a local public library. Public libraries usually have a large reference section with many resources available for loan, including CD-ROMs, encyclopaedias, government statistics, magazines, journals and newspapers, and databases such as Infotrac, which contains articles from newspapers and magazines over the last five years.

The librarian will show you how to find the resources you need and how to look up a specific book (or author) to check if it is available or is out on loan.

TRY THIS

Schedule your research time by calculating backwards from the deadline date. Split the time you have 50/50 between searching for information and using it. This stops you searching for too long and getting lots of interesting material, but then not having the time to use it properly!

Some books and resources can only be used in the library itself, while others can be taken out on short-term or long-term loan. You need to plan how to access and use the resources that are popular or restricted.

Using your library

✔ If your centre has an intranet you might be able to check which books and CD-ROMs are available without actually visiting the library.

✔ All libraries have photocopying facilities, so take enough change with you to copy articles that you can't remove. Write down the source of any article you photocopy, ie the name and the date of the publication.

✔ Learn how to keep a reference file (or bibliography) in which you store the details of all your sources and references. A bibliography must include CDs, DVDs and other information formats, not just books and magazines.

✔ If your search is complicated, go at a quiet time when the librarian can help you.

✔ Don't get carried away if you find several books that contain the information you need. Too many can be confusing.

✔ Use the index to find information quickly by searching for key words. Scan the index using several likely alternatives.

✔ Only use books that you find easy to understand. A book is only helpful if you can retell the information in your own words.

Researching online

A good search engine such as Google will help you find useful websites. They look for sites based on the information you enter in the search box. In some cases, such as Ask.co.uk, you may get the chance to refine your choice after entering your key words or question.

Finding information on a website

Wikipedia is a popular free online encyclopaedia. It has been criticised because entries may be inaccurate as members of the public can edit the site. However, Wikipedia is trying to prevent this by organising professional editing.

If you're not sure whether something you read is correct, or if there is anything strange about it, check it against information on another site. Make sure you ask your tutor's opinion, too.

With large websites, it can be difficult to find what you need. Always read the whole screen – there may be several menus in different parts of the screen.

To help you search, many large websites have:

- their own search facility or a site map that lists site content with links to the different pages
- links to similar sites where you might find more information. Clicking a link should open a new window, so you'll still be connected to the original site.

TRY THIS

Search engines don't just find websites. On Google, the options at the top of your screen include 'images', 'news' and 'maps'. If you click on 'more' and then 'even more', you'll find other options, too. You'll usually find the most relevant information if you use the UK version of a search engine. Only search the whole web if you deliberately want to include European and American information. Go to page 90 to find out how you can see this in action.

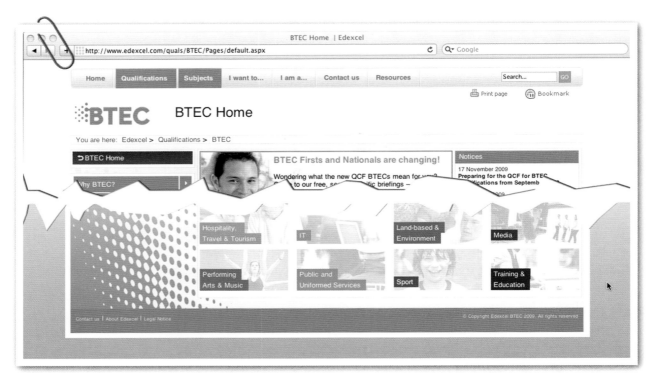

There may be useful information and links at the top, foot or either side of a web page.

There are several other useful sites you could visit when researching online.
- **Directory sites** show websites in specific categories so you can focus your search at the start.
- **Forums** are sites, or areas of a website, where people post comments on an issue. They can be useful if you want to find out opinions on a topic. You can usually read them without registering.
- **News sites** include the BBC website as well as the sites for all the daily newspapers. Check the website of your local newspaper, too.

Printing information
- Only print information that you're sure will be useful. It's easy to print too much and find yourself drowning in paper.
- Make quick notes on your print-outs so that you remember why you wanted them. It will jog your memory when you're sorting through them later.
- If there's a printer-friendly option, use it. It will give you a print-out without unnecessary graphics or adverts.
- Check the bottom line of your print-outs. It should show the URL for that page of the website, and the date. You need those if you have to list your sources or if you want to quote from the page.

TRY THIS

To see how directory sites work go to page 90.

TOP TIPS

Bookmark sites you use regularly by adding the URL to your browser. How to do this will depend on which browser you use, eg Internet Explorer, Firefox.

Researching by asking other people

You're likely to do this for two reasons:

- you need help from someone who knows a lot about a topic
- you need to find out several people's opinions on something.

Information from an expert

Explain politely why you are carrying out the investigation. Ask questions slowly and clearly about what they do and how they do it. If they don't mind, you could take written notes so you remember what they tell you. Put the name and title of the person, and the date, at the top. This is especially important if you might be seeing more than one person, to avoid getting your notes muddled up.

Ask whether you may contact them again, in case there's anything you need to check. Write down their phone number or email address. Above all, remember to say 'thank you'!

Reasons for research

Research on a BTEC First in Health and Social Care can be carried out for a number of different reasons. You might be asked to research:

- the different health and social care settings in your local area
- the roles and responsibilities associated with a particular job role in a drug rehabilitation centre for inclusion in a magazine article about the vocation.

Some of the research you will undertake will be done individually. However, many projects will involve research carried out in small groups with the results shared with the whole team.

Case study: Finding the information you need

Students at St Mary's High School are working on a public health campaign. They are creating a short activity session to raise awareness of the importance of healthy eating among five to seven year-olds as part of the units on The Impact of Diet on Health and Creative and Therapeutic Activities in Health and Social Care

The project involves a number of research tasks, which the group are intending to share across the team.

Anwar and Helena are going to undertake an investigation into the messages communicated in existing healthy eating campaigns, particularly those aimed at families and young children. They will do this by searching the internet and collecting leaflets from places such as health centres.

Clare and Dwayne are going to investigate how school dinners can contribute to healthy eating for children. They will begin by interviewing the catering manager at their own school.

Ivan, Rachel and Eloise are aiming to find out about the needs of the target audience. They have arranged to go to a local primary school to get tips from the teaching staff about producing educational materials for the five to seven age range.

Finally, Harley, Rhys and Ebony are going to find out about the work of companies involved in existing healthy eating campaigns. They are beginning their investigations by searching the internet and they hope to be able to arrange interviews with members of some of the companies they find out about.

The opinions of several people

The easiest way to do this is with a questionnaire. You can either give people the questionnaire to complete themselves or interview them and complete it yourself. Professional interviewers often telephone people to ask questions, but at this stage it's not a good idea unless you know the people you're phoning and they're happy for you to do this.

Devising a questionnaire

1. Make sure it has a title and clear instructions.

2. Rather than ask for opinions, give people options, eg yes/no, maybe/always, never/sometimes. This will make it easier to analyse the results.

3. Or you can ask interviewees to give a score, say out of 5, making it clear what each number represents, eg 5 = excellent, 4 = very good.

4. Keep your questionnaire short so that your interviewees don't lose interest. Between 10 and 15 questions is probably about right, as long as that's enough to find out all you need.

5. Remember to add 'thank you' at the end.

6. Decide upon the representative sample of people you will approach. These are the people whose views are the most relevant to the topic you're investigating.

7. Decide how many responses you need to get a valid answer. This means that the answer is representative of the wider population. For example, if you want views on food in your canteen, it's pointless only asking five people. You might pick the only five people who detest (or love) the food it serves.

TOP TIPS

Design your questionnaire so that you get quantifiable answers. This means you can easily add them up to get your final result.

TRY THIS

Always test your draft questionnaire on several people, to highlight any confusing questions or instructions.

Keeping a logbook

A logbook can be used to document the range and amount of vocational experience you have undertaken. The studying of some units requires evidence of you having completed a number of hours of vocational experience (you should check with your tutor if you are unsure).

The logbook should include notes taken during your vocational experience lessons, diary entries for each day on a placement, for example giving accounts of what went well or badly, with reasons why; summary of guest speakers; images; ideas and anything else which might help you develop your work. It would also be worth looking at how your vocational experiences relate to the units you are studying, such as the health and safety requirements of the placement or perhaps the needs of the service users.

Complete the logbook regularly to make sure the work you have undertaken is fresh in your mind.

Below is an example from a vocational experience logbook produced by a learner undertaking Unit 5 Vocational Experience in a Health or Social Care Setting as part of her BTEC First in Health and Social Care.

Phoebe Dean Vocational experience: Curly Caterpillars Day Nursery, 3rd March 2009
Summary of work undertaken so far
I have just finished my second day on my vocational experience and I absolutely love it! I am placed at a nursery and the staff are really friendly. I am working with two to three year-olds and there are about 10 children who come in the morning and eight in the afternoon. We sing songs like 'The Wheels on the Bus' and 'The Colours of the Rainbow'. I have also read books to a small group of children and done some painting with another group. It is hard work clearing up at the end of each session as they make so much mess! I didn't really think we would have to clear up, but it makes sense I suppose!
What went well? What went badly? What have you learnt?
When I was reading a book to the children, some were getting a bit restless. I wondered why this was and thought it might have been because I didn't show the children any pictures. I think if I read books again to the children, I will show them the pictures to keep their attention.

Do you think the headings have helped Phoebe to keep her comments focused while completing her logbook?

Activity: Using resources effectively

Use the table below to show what you think the pros and cons of each resource are.

	Textbook	Newspaper	Website	Magazine	Television programme
PROS					
CONS					

Managing your information

Whether you've found lots of information or only a little, assessing what you have and using it wisely is very important. This section will help you avoid the main pitfalls.

Organising and selecting your information

Organising your information

The first step is to organise your information so that it's easy to use.

- Make sure your written notes are neat and have a clear heading – it's often useful to date them, too.
- Note useful pages in any books or magazines you have borrowed.
- Highlight relevant parts of any handouts or leaflets.
- Work out the results of any questionnaires you've used.

Selecting your information

Re-read the **assignment brief** or instructions you were given to remind yourself of the exact wording of the question(s) and divide your information into three groups:

1. Information that is totally relevant.
2. Information that is not as good, but could come in useful.
3. Information that doesn't match the questions or assignment brief very much but that you kept because you couldn't find anything better!

Check there are no obvious gaps in your information against the questions or assignment brief. If there are, make a note of them so that you know exactly what you still have to find. Although it's ideal to have everything you need before you start work, don't delay if you're short of time.

Putting your information in order

Putting your information in a logical order means you can find what you want easily. It will also save you time in the long run, which is doubly important if you are accumulating lots of information and will be doing the work over several sessions.

Case study: Organising your research

Charlie reflects on his organisational skills over the duration of his BTEC course.

'My tutor advised us at the beginning of the course that we would need to be well organised with our work. She said it would be a good idea to purchase a folder and dividers so we could store our class notes under the appropriate unit headings.

I had every intention of going home and filing my class notes and, for the first couple of weeks, I did this. However, I soon became slack and stopped filing my notes away. A pile soon built up at the front of my folder and my notes kept falling out.

When it came to writing my assignments, my tutor told us to use our class notes to help, but I had no idea which notes were for which unit, assignment or task! My assignments ended up being really confused and my tutor asked me what was going on as my work appeared unorganised.

We sat down and went through my folder, sorting out which units the notes were from. She also encouraged me to write the date, unit, assignment and task on the notes every time I make them, so even if I don't file them straight away, I at least know where they belong when I come to use them later.

I now feel much better organised and have started adding extra research to my folder which I think may be useful for future assignments, such as newspaper articles and a list of books I thought were good. I am really proud of my folder now and my work is a lot more structured as a result.'

TOP TIPS

Add a separate section to your ring binder for any important information regarding your Health and Social Care assignments, including the hand-in dates and useful websites.

Activity: Techniques for making notes

You will be expected to make notes independently during lessons. Sometimes it can be hard to keep up with the flow in class, especially in discussion based lessons, if you are constantly writing. To increase your writing speed when you are making notes, it can be helpful to use abbreviations.

Which abbreviations do/can you use? Make a list of your abbreviations below. This is a personal list, so don't be worried if your abbreviations are different to someone else's. Use the examples to start you off.

Phrase	Abbreviation
for example	eg
remember	nb
health and social care	H+SC

In the case study above, Charlie stored his notes in unit order. How do you store yours? Chronologically, numerically, alphabetically?

Any other way?

Interpreting and presenting your information

The next stage is to use your information to prepare the document and/or oral presentation you have to give. There are four steps:

1 Understand what you're reading.
2 Interpret what you're reading.
3 Know the best form in which to produce the information, bearing in mind the purpose for which it is required.
4 Create the required document so that it's in a suitable layout with correct spelling and punctuation.

Understanding what you read

As a general rule, never use information that you don't understand. However, nobody understands complex or unfamiliar material the first time they read it, especially if they just scan through it quickly. Before you reject it, try this:

Read it once to get the main idea.	→ Read it again, slowly, to try to take in more detail.	→ Look up any words you don't know in a dictionary to find out what they mean.
Write your own version.	← Summarise the main points in your own words.	← Read it a third time and underline or highlight the main points. (If this is a book or magazine that you shouldn't write in, take a photocopy first and write on that.)

Special note: Show both the article and your own version to your tutor to check your understanding. This will help you identify any points you missed out and help you improve your skills of interpreting and summarising.

Understanding unfamiliar information

BTEC FACT

In your assignments, it's better to separate opinions from facts. If you're quoting someone's views, make this clear. (See also page 56.)

Interpreting what you read

Interpreting what you read is different from understanding it. This is because you can't always take it for granted that something you read means what it says. The writer may have had a very strong or biased opinion, or may have exaggerated for effect. This doesn't mean that you can't use the information.

Strong opinions and bias

People often have strong points of view about certain topics. This may be based on reliable facts, but not always! We can all jump to conclusions that may not be very logical, especially if we feel strongly about something.

Things aren't always what they seem to be. Are these boys fighting or are they having a good time?

Exaggeration

Many newspapers exaggerate facts to startle and attract their readers.

LOCAL FIRM DOUBLES STAFF IN TWO WEEKS!

This newspaper headline sounds very positive. You could easily think it means employment is growing and there are more jobs in your area. Then you read on, and find the firm had only four staff and now has eight!

Tables and graphs

You need to be able to interpret what the figures mean, especially when you look at differences between columns or rows. For example, your friend might have an impressive spreadsheet that lists his income and expenditure. In reality, it doesn't tell you much until you add the figures up and subtract one from the other. Only then can you say whether he is getting into debt. And even if he is, you need to see his budget over a few months, rather than just one which may be exceptional.

Choosing a format

You may have been given specific instructions about the format and layout of a document you have to produce, in which case life is easy as long as you follow them! If not, think carefully about the best way to set out your information so that it is clear.

TRY THIS

There are many scare stories in the media about issues such as immigration, children's reading ability or obesity. Next time you're watching television and these are discussed, see if you can spot biased views, exaggeration and claims without any supporting evidence.

TOP TIPS

Never make assumptions or jump to conclusions. Make sure you have all the evidence to support your views.

Different formats	Example
text	when you write in paragraphs or prepare a report or summary
graphical	a diagram, graph or chart
pictorial	a drawing, photograph, cartoon or pictogram
tabular	numerical information in a table

The best method(s) will depend on the information you have, the source(s) of your material and the purpose of the document – a leaflet for schoolchildren needs graphics and pictures to make it lively, whereas a report to company shareholders would be mainly in text form with just one or two graphs.

Stating your sources

Whatever format you use, if you are including other people's views, comments or opinions, or copying a table or diagram from another publication, you must state the source by including the name of the author, publication or the web address. This can be in the text or as part of a list at the end. Failure to do this (so you are really pretending other people's work is your own) is known as **plagiarism**. It is a serious offence with penalties to match.

Text format

Creating written documents gets easier with practice. These points should help.

TOP TIPS

Don't just rely on your spellchecker. It won't find a word spelled wrongly that makes another valid word (eg from/form), so you must proofread everything. And remember to check whether it is set to check American English or British English. There are some spelling differences.

Golden rules for written documents

1 Think about who will be reading it, then write in an appropriate language and style.

2 Ensure it is technically correct, ie no wrong spellings or bad punctuation.

3 Take time to make it look good, with clear headings, consistent spacing and plenty of white space.

4 Write in paragraphs, each with a different theme. Leave a line space between each one.

5 If you have a lot of separate points to mention, use bullets or numbered points. Numbered points show a certain order or quantity (step 1, step 2, etc). Use bullet points when there is no suggested order.

6 Only use words that you understand the meaning of, or it might look as if you don't know what you mean.

7 Structure your document so that it has a beginning, middle and end.

8 Prepare a draft and ask your tutor to confirm you are on the right track and are using your information in the best way.

Graphical format

TRY THIS

Someone asks for directions to your house. Would you write a list or draw a diagram? Which would be easier for you and for the other person – and why?

Most people find graphics better than a long description for creating a quick picture in the viewer's mind. There are several types of graphical format, and you can easily produce any of these if you have good ICT skills.

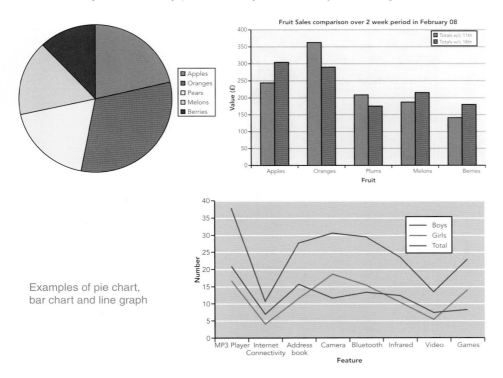

Examples of pie chart, bar chart and line graph

Pictorial format

Newspapers and magazines use pictures to illustrate situations and reduce the amount of words needed. It doesn't always have to be photographs though. For example, a new building may be sketched to show what it will look like.

A pictogram or pictograph is another type of pictorial format, such as charts which use the image of an object (fruit, coins, even pizzas) to represent data, such as the number eaten or amount spent.

TOP TIPS

Don't spend hours writing text when an illustration can do the job better – but make sure the illustration you choose is suitable for the document and the reader.

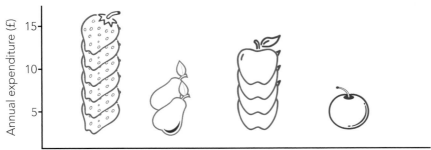

Tabular format

A table can be an easy way to communicate information. Imagine a retailer preparing information about the items in stock. Text would be difficult to understand and comparisons between stock levels and sales would be almost impossible to make. A table, however, would easily show the fastest-selling items.

Tables are also ideal if you are showing rankings – such as best-selling music or books.

Bestsellers list – September 2009

Position	Title	Author	Imprint	Publication
1 (New)	Lost Symbol,The	Brown, Dan	Bantam Press	15-Sep-2009
2 (1)	Complaints, The	Rankin, Ian	Orion	03-Sep-2009
3 (New)	Return Journey, The	Binchy, Maeve	Orion	17-Sep-2009
4 (7)	Sapphire	Price, Katie	Century	30-Jul-2009
5 (9)	Wolf Hall	Mantel, Hilary	Fourth Estate	30-Apr-2009
6 (3)	Week in December, A	Faulks, Sebastian	Hutchinson	03-Sep-2009
7 (2)	Alex Cross's Trial	Patterson, James	Century	10-Sep-2009
8 (4)	White Queen, The	Gregory, Philippa	Simon & Schuster Ltd	18-Aug-2009
9 (5)	Even Money	Francis, Dick & Francis, Felix	Michael Joseph	03-Sep-2009
10 (8)	206 Bones	Reichs, Kathy	William Heinemann	27-Aug-2009

National newspaper circulation – September 2009

	August 2009	August 2008	% change on last year	August 09 (without bulks)	March 2009 – August 2009	% change on last year
Sun	3,128,501	3,148,792	-0.64	3,128,501	3,052,480	-2.25
Daily Mail	2,171,686	2,258,843	-3.86	2,044,079	2,178,462	-4.45
Daily Mirror	1,324,883	1,455,270	-8.96	1,324,883	1,331,108	9.44
Daily Star	886,814	751,494	18.01	886,814	855,511	16.65
The Daily Telegraph	814,087	860,298	-5.37	722,644	807,328	-6.73
Daily Express	730,234	748,664	-2.46	730,234	727,824	-1.32
Times	576,185	612,779	-5.97	529,746	588,471	-4.63
Financial Times	395,845	417,570	-5.2	365,269	411,098	-6.7
Daily Record	347,302	390,197	-10.99	345,277	350,306	-10.59
Guardian	311,387	332,587	-6.37	311,387	332,790	-4.11
Independent	187,837	230,033	-18.34	148,551	198,445	-16.76

Activity: Presenting your information

Your BTEC First in Health and Social Care will require you to present a variety of information for many different reasons. Match each piece of presented information to its correct format.

Presented information		Format
Service users and their blood groups		text
Cross-section of the heart		graphical
Scientific report		graphical
Photograph		text
Service users and their health requirements		pictorial
Pie chart		tabular
Newspaper article		pictorial
Scatter graph		graphical
Cartoon		tabular

Activity: Choosing an appropriate format to present

Which type of format do you think would be best for presenting the information in the table? Choose from the following formats:

- text
- graphical (including spidergrams)
- pictorial
- tabular.

Type of information	Format
The results of a service user survey about an activity you carried out with them.	
Information gathered about the life of a health or social care practitioner.	
The results of an audit into the number of people who smoke (and how many cigarettes a day) on your course.	
Ideas for uniforms to wear on vocational experience.	
A list of the typical job roles to be found in a hospital and how they relate to one another.	
Information about the number of raffle tickets sold for three charity events, raising money for the homeless.	

Making presentations

Presentations help you to learn communication skills.

Some people hate the idea of standing up to speak in front of an audience. This is quite normal, and you can use the extra energy from nerves to improve your performance.

Presentations aren't some form of torture devised by your tutor! They are included in your course because they help you learn many skills, such as speaking in public and preparing visual aids. They also help you practise working as a team member and give you a practical reason for researching information. And it can be far more enjoyable to talk about what you've found out rather than write about it!

There's a knack to preparing and giving a presentation so that you use your energies well, don't waste time, don't fall out with everyone around you and keep your stress levels as low as possible. Think about the task in three stages: preparation, organisation and delivery.

Preparation

Start your initial preparations as soon as you can. Putting them off will only cause problems later. Discuss the task in your team so that everyone is clear about what has to be done and how long you have to do it in.

Divide any research fairly among the team, allowing for people's strengths and weaknesses. You'll also need to agree:

- which visual aids would be best
- which handouts you need and who should prepare them
- where and when the presentation will be held, and what you should wear
- what questions you might be asked, both individually and as a team, and how you should prepare for them.

Once you've decided all this, carry out the tasks you've been allocated to the best of your ability and by the deadline agreed.

TOP TIPS

Keep visual aids simple but effective and check any handouts carefully before you make lots of copies.

Organisation

This is about the planning you need to do as a team so that everything will run smoothly on the day.

Delivery

Presenting and sharing work with other learners will be a regular activity on your BTEC First in Health and Social Care. Whether you are delivering a PowerPoint presentation about a religion or secular belief you have researched or sharing a creative or therapeutic activity you have created.

Case study: Ready to present?

The BTEC First in Health and Social Care learners at South Hampshire College are undertaking their second assignment. While the first assignment required them as a whole class to prepare and carry out a display on the lifespan and development of an individual, the second assignment is very different. The class started off together, discussing effective communication.

They were then asked to work in groups of four to develop a talk show focusing on communication techniques and present it to the rest of the class. They were also asked to be prepared to discuss the work and receive feedback from the other learners.

The fact they knew their work would be discussed by the class and possibly criticised made a lot of the learners nervous.

Whenever you take part in a session like this, try to put your fellow learners at ease. If you are watching a presentation:

- remember that criticism should always be constructive; don't simply say you didn't like something, but try to explain how it might have been improved
- try to find something good to say to balance out any negative comments.

If you are presenting work:

- try not to take criticism personally. It is the work, not you as a person, that is being discussed!

TOP TIPS

Never read from prepared prompt cards! Look at the audience when you're talking and smile occasionally. If you need to use prompt cards as a reminder, write clearly so that you need only glance at them.

TOP TIPS

Remember the audience always makes allowances for some nerves!

Activity: Preparing, delivering and watching presentations

How well will you cope with the presentations you will have to take part in on your BTEC First in Health and Social Care?

This quiz should get you thinking!

1 You have just finished your presentation on the importance of avoiding discrimination in a health and social care setting. Someone in your class asks a question you don't know the answer to. Do you:

- **a)** try to avoid the question by changing the subject?
- **b)** admit that you don't know the answer?
- **c)** make something up, hoping they'll never realise?

2 A learner on your course is delivering a presentation and he is obviously very nervous. Do you:

- **a)** sink into your chair with embarrassment?
- **b)** look at him and smile in an encouraging way?
- **c)** try to think of a difficult question to ask at the end?

3 It's the day before an important presentation and you've forgotten to book a place in the computer suite. This means there is no way you'll get your PowerPoint finished in time. Do you:

- **a)** pretend to be unwell?
- **b)** come clean, apologise and try to get through the presentation anyway?
- **c)** blame someone else?

4 The class has been divided into groups and asked to come up with ideas for a Christmas event which your class will be running for the local nursery. When the time comes to present and share your ideas, you discover the first group has come up with a very similar idea to the one your group has chosen. Do you:

- **a)** make an excuse and go to the toilet when it's your group's turn?
- **b)** present your idea anyway?
- **c)** accuse the other group of stealing your idea?

5 You have been working as part of a group coming up with and developing ideas for a presentation on laws and legislations. One member of your group has not been pulling her weight and as the presentation approaches you are worried that it will affect the group's performance. Do you:

- **a)** cross your fingers and hope she doesn't turn up for the presentation?
- **b)** talk to your tutor and ask their advice?
- **c)** lose your temper with her and tell her not to bother turning up on the day?

To find out how you did, see page 90.

Your assessments

The importance of assignments

All learners on BTEC First courses are assessed by means of **assignments**. Each one is designed to link to specific **learning outcomes** and **grading criteria**. At the end of the course, your assignment grades put together determine your overall grade.

To get the best grade you can, you need to know the golden rules that apply to all assignments, then how to interpret the specific instructions.

10 golden rules for assignments

1. Check that you understand the instructions.

2. Check whether you have to do all the work on your own, or if you will do some as a member of a group. If you work as a team, you need to identify which parts are your own contributions.

3. Always write down any verbal instructions you are given.

4. Check the final deadline and any penalties for not meeting it.

5. Make sure you know what to do if you have a serious personal problem, eg illness, and need an official extension.

6. Copying someone else's work (**plagiarism**) is a serious offence and is easy for experienced tutors to spot. It's never worth the risk.

7. Schedule enough time for finding out the information and doing initial planning.

8. Allow plenty of time between talking to your tutor about your plans, preparations and drafts and the final deadline.

9. Don't panic if the assignment seems long or complicated. Break it down into small, manageable chunks.

10. If you suddenly get stuck, ask your tutor to talk things through with you.

Case study: Understanding assessment

Skyla gets feedback from her first assignment.

'My first assignment for my BTEC First in Health and Social Care was completed last week and ever since I handed it in I have been a bit anxious about how I have done.

In today's lesson we were each given an assessment feedback sheet for the assignment. It was more detailed than I had expected and really helped me to understand how I had done and what I need to do to get a better grade next time.

The assignment was for Unit 7 Anatomy and Physiology for Health and Social Care and was in two parts. In the first part we had to identify and briefly describe different muscles in the human body. I found out about the muscles in the leg and described how they help us to walk and run. I presented my findings using PowerPoint. In the second part of the assignment we had to pick a body organ and make a drawing of it and label its functions. Then we had to write a scientific report discussing what would happen if we didn't have the organ and why it is important.

I was more worried about the second part of the assignment and when I got the feedback I was really pleased to have achieved a merit for the task. The assessment feedback sheet gave details about where I had done well and also included advice on how to improve and achieve a distinction which I missed out on for the second task. The tutor has given us another deadline to repeat the scientific report and hand it in, so I am hoping to improve my grade to a distinction on my resubmission.'

Interpreting the instructions

Most assignments start with a **command word** – describe, explain, evaluate, etc. These words relate to how complex the answer should be.

Command words

Learners often don't do their best because they read the command words but don't understand exactly what they have to do. The following tables show you what is required for each grade when you see a particular command word.

Command words and obtaining a pass

Complete ...	Complete a form, diagram or drawing.
Demonstrate ...	Show that you can do a particular activity.
Describe ...	Give a clear, straightforward description that includes all the main points.
Identify ...	Give all the basic facts relating to a certain topic.
List ...	Write a list of the main items (not sentences).
Name ...	State the proper terms related to a drawing or diagram.
Outline ...	Give all the main points, but without going into too much detail.
State ...	Point out or list the main features.

Examples:
- **List** the main features on your mobile phone.
- **Describe** the best way to greet a customer.
- **Outline** the procedures you follow to keep your computer system secure.

Command words and obtaining a merit

Analyse ...	Identify the factors that apply, and state how these are linked and how each of them relates to the topic.
Comment on ...	Give your own opinions or views.
Compare ... **Contrast ...**	Identify the main factors relating to two or more items and point out the similarities and differences.
Competently use ...	Take full account of information and feedback you have obtained to review or improve an activity.
Demonstrate ...	Prove you can carry out a more complex activity.
Describe ...	Give a full description including details of all the relevant features.
Explain ...	Give logical reasons to support your views.
Justify ...	Give reasons for the points you are making so that the reader knows what you're thinking.
Suggest ...	Give your own ideas or thoughts.

Examples:
- **Explain** why mobile phones are so popular.
- **Describe** the needs of four different types of customers.
- **Suggest** the type of procedures your employer would need to introduce to keep the IT system secure.

Command words and obtaining a distinction

Analyse ...	Identify several relevant factors, show how they are linked, and explain the importance of each.
Compare ... **Contrast ...**	Identify the main factors in two or more situations, then explain the similarities and differences, and in some cases say which is best and why.
Demonstrate ...	Prove that you can carry out a complex activity taking into account information you have obtained or received to adapt your original idea.
Describe ...	Give a comprehensive description which tells a story to the reader and shows that you can apply your knowledge and information correctly.
Evaluate ...	Bring together all your information and make a judgement on the importance or success of something.
Explain ...	Provide full details and reasons to support the arguments you are making.
Justify ...	Give full reasons or evidence to support your opinion.
Recommend ...	Weigh up all the evidence to come to a conclusion, with reasons, about what would be best.

Examples:
- **Evaluate** the features and performance of your mobile phone.
- **Analyse** the role of customer service in contributing to an organisation's success.
- **Justify** the main features on the website of a large, successful organisation of your choice.

TRY THIS

Check the command word you are likely to see for each of your units in the **grading grid** in advance. This tells you the **grading criteria** for the unit so that you know the evidence you will have to present.

TOP TIPS

Think of assignments as an opportunity to demonstrate what you've learned and to get useful feedback on your work.

Activity: Getting the best result

Learners at St George's Community College are completing an assignment for the Ensuring Safe Environments in Health and Social Care unit. The task they are completing requires them to plan and carry out a risk assessment of their work experience placement.

The **pass** criterion requires learners to:
- plan a risk assessment in a health or social care environment.

The **merit** criterion asks them to:
- carry out a risk assessment in a health or social care environment.

The **distinction** criterion asks them to:
- present a persuasive case for action based on the findings of their risk assessment.

Caitlin makes a risk assessment grid to complete when she is on her work placement that spots hazards and safety issues. Unfortunately, Caitlin is ill during her work experience and she does not complete the grid and hands it in uncompleted.

Ajit provides a detailed table which he completes during his placement. He uses the information to assess the different hazards and safety issues accurately. He also uses it to write a detailed report, discussing ways to overcome the hazards by suggesting sensible ideas to make the setting safer.

Grace produces a well thought out risk assessment which she completes to a high standard, describing the risks and hazards effectively. She attempts to produce a report, giving ideas for ways to overcome the hazards and risks, but her answers are limited and unrealistic.

a) Who do you think has done enough to achieve a distinction?

b) Who would be given a merit?

c) Who would be marked at a pass?

Activity: Command words wordsearch

Which command word best matches the following definitions? You will find them all in the wordsearch below.

a) Show differences when compared, using examples where appropriate.

b) Discuss the reason for something, how it works and how to do something.

c) Show how relevant factors are linked and relate to the topic.

d) Give a good and acceptable reason for something.

e) Describe roughly or briefly or give the main points or summary of an idea or argument.

f) Examine and note the similarities or differences, using examples where appropriate.

g) Say or write something; express in words.

h) List, recognise and name.

i) Show what something is by drawing a picture with words.

j) Discuss the pros and cons and give suggestions for improvements.

E	S	Y	L	A	N	A	X	I	E
V	I	Y	F	I	T	S	U	J	R
A	N	F	L	I	A	E	A	C	A
L	I	S	O	S	T	T	O	L	P
U	A	A	E	U	S	N	R	E	M
A	L	U	R	J	T	U	E	J	O
T	P	J	S	R	O	L	C	D	C
E	X	A	A	A	M	V	I	O	I
D	E	S	C	R	I	B	E	N	D
D	T	R	T	E	S	T	A	T	E

You can find the answers on page 90.

Sample assignment

Note about assignments

All learners are different and will approach their assignment in different ways.
The sample assignment that follows shows how one learner answered a brief to achieve pass, merit and distinction level criteria. The learner work shows just one way in which grading criteria can be evidenced. There are no standard or set answers. If you produce the required evidence for each task then you will achieve the grading criteria covered by the assignment.

Front sheet

Make sure that you complete the front sheet fully, accurately and neatly. Fill in all the boxes and spaces. Write your name in full.

Hand work in before or on the set completion date. Find out about the centre policy on meeting deadlines.

Before submitting your work, ask your assessor to check it is all there. You may have forgotten some evidence.

This table tells you what evidence you must produce to achieve the criteria. Your assessor will tell you what to do to achieve this.

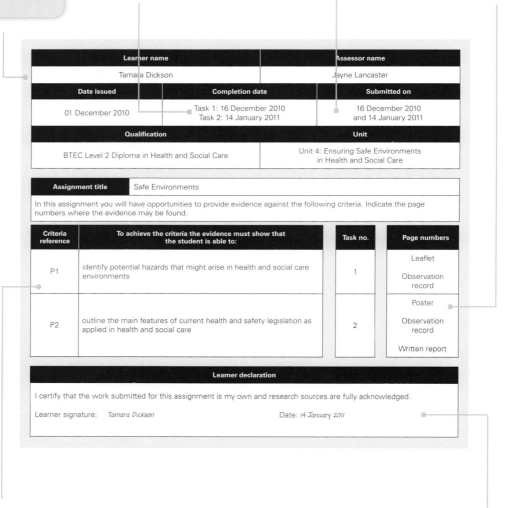

Learner name			Assessor name	
Tamara Dickson			Jayne Lancaster	
Date issued	**Completion date**		**Submitted on**	
01 December 2010	Task 1: 16 December 2010 Task 2: 14 January 2011		16 December 2010 and 14 January 2011	
Qualification			**Unit**	
BTEC Level 2 Diploma in Health and Social Care			Unit 4: Ensuring Safe Environments in Health and Social Care	

Assignment title	Safe Environments

In this assignment you will have opportunities to provide evidence against the following criteria. Indicate the page numbers where the evidence may be found.

Criteria reference	To achieve the criteria the evidence must show that the student is able to:	Task no.	Page numbers
P1	identify potential hazards that might arise in health and social care environments	1	Leaflet Observation record
P2	outline the main features of current health and safety legislation as applied in health and social care	2	Poster Observation record Written report

Learner declaration
I certify that the work submitted for this assignment is my own and research sources are fully acknowledged. Learner signature: *Tamara Dickson*   Date: *14 January 2011*

For a particular criterion, check that your evidence adequately covers the topics which are in the unit content range statement. You can ask your assessor to check for you.

Make sure that any evidence you present is your own and not copied from other people's work. Acknowledge any information you used at the end of your work by referencing.

Assignment brief

By relating the assignment tasks to health and social care settings, scenarios help you solve some problems that you could face in the real world of health and social care.

When completing the assignment, remember the title as this can help you stay focused and on the right path.

Unit title	Unit 4: Ensuring Safe Environments in Health and Social Care	
Qualification	BTEC Level 2 Diploma in Health and Social Care	
Start date	01 December 2010	
Deadline date	Task 1: 16 December 2010 Task 2: 14 January 2011	
Assessor	Jayne Lancaster	
Assignment title	Safe Environments	

The purpose of this assignment is to:
enable learners to gain knowledge of potential hazards in health and social care environments, and to know the main principles of health and safety legislation applied to health and social care environments.

Scenario
You are working at a care home and one of your roles is that of the health and safety co-ordinator. You have noticed that the health and safety displays and information booklets for staff and service users are very shabby and need to be refreshed and updated.

Task 1
You are to produce a staff leaflet identifying potential hazards in health and social care environments.

Your tutor/assessor will look at your completed leaflet and will fill in an observation record as evidence that you have produced this and also to confirm that it identifies the potential hazards in health and social care environments.

This provides evidence for P1

Task 2
a) You will be divided into pairs and each pair will be given a piece of legislation to look at in relation to health and social care settings. Research this legislation and produce a poster. You will then need to present your poster to the rest of the group. All BTEC evidence must be individual, even if the work involved in producing it was done in a group.

Your tutor/assessor will look at your completed poster and will complete an observation record statement as evidence that you have produced your poster and that it outlines the main principles of a current health and safety legislation applied to health and social care environments.

b) You will also need to observe presentations by others in the group on other legislations, and you will need to prepare a written outline of the key points of each piece of legislations, including their strengths and weaknesses.

This provides evidence for P2

Key Terms:

Observation Record = Your assessor will confirm that you have completed the set work competently by filling in an observation record.

Present = Discussing your work with the rest of the class and telling them about your work in a formal manner.

Individual = Completing work on your own.

Group = Working as a group to produce a piece of work, but providing individual contributions.

Don't just rely on the internet when you are researching. Books can be helpful, particularly ones written specifically for your course.

Sources of information

Asbridge L, Lavers S, Moonie N and Scott J – *BTEC First Health and Social Care* (Heinemann, 2006) ISBN 0435463322

Clarke L – *Health and Social Care GCSE* (Nelson Thornes, 2002) ISBN 0748770720

Eden S – *Society, Health and Development Level 1 Foundation Diploma* (Pearson, 2008) ISBN 9780435500900

Haworth E, Allen B, Forshaw C, Nicol D, Volbracht A and Leach J – *Society, Health and Development Level 2 Higher Diploma* (Pearson, 2008) ISBN 9780435401030

Learning and Skills Council – *Standards for Health and Safety*

Pritchard J and Kemshall H (editors) – *Good Practice in Risk Assessment and Risk Management* (Jessica Kingsley, 1995) ISBN 9781853023385

Spencer R and Fisher I – *The Essentials of Health and Safety (Carers)* (Highfield Publications) ISBN 1871912032

Websites

www.bohs.org – British Occupational Hygiene Society

www.cqc.org.uk – Care Quality Commission

www.doh.gov.uk – Department of Health

www.foodstandards.gov.uk – Food Standards Agency

www.hse.gov.uk – Health and Safety Executive

This brief has beeen verified as being fit for purpose			
Assessor	Jayne Lancaster		
Signature	*Jayne Lancaster*	**Date**	*19 November 2010*
Internal verifier	George Brennan		
Signature	*George Brennan*	**Date**	*19 November 2010*

Sample learner work

The leaflet has been given a title which helps the learners to remember what their leaflet should contain.

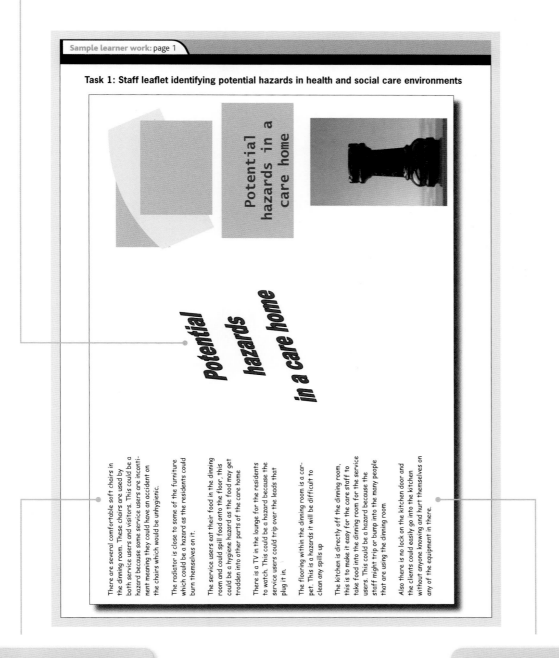

Sample learner work: page 1

Task 1: Staff leaflet identifying potential hazards in health and social care environments

Potential hazards in a care home

There are several comfortable soft chairs in the dinning room. These chairs are used by both service users and visitors. This could be a hazard because some service users are incontinent meaning they could have an accident on the chairs which would be unhygienic.

The radiator is close to some of the furniture which could be a hazard as the residents could burn themselves on it.

The service users eat their food in the dinning room and could spill food onto the floor, this could be a hygiene hazard as the food may get trodden into other parts of the care home

There is a TV in the lounge for the residents to watch. This could be a hazard because the service users could trip over the leads that plug it in.

The flooring within the dinning room is a carpet. This is a hazards it will be difficult to clean any spills up

The kitchen is directly off the dinning room, this is to make it easy for the care staff to take food into the dinning room for the service users. This could be a hazard because the staff might trip or bump into the many people that are using the dinning room

Also there is no lock on the kitchen door and the clients could easily go into the kitchen without anyone knowing and hurt themselves on any of the equipment in there.

Good, simple statements which are easy to read and understand. The evidence meets the requirements of the grading criteria because description is not required.

The leaflet has been presented in a clear format with separate paragraphs for each hazard. These could have been bullet pointed to improve the layout.

The floor plan shows all the furniture and items in the home. They could be numbered and matched to the hazards to make it easier to read.

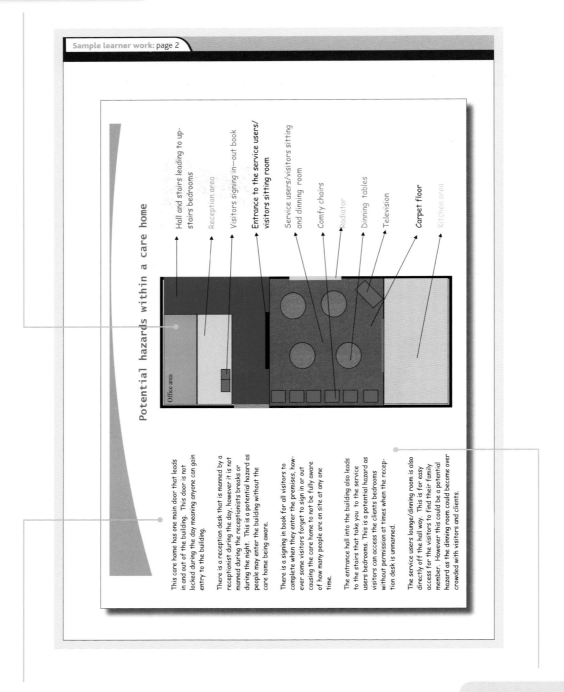

Sample learner work: page 2

Potential hazards within a care home

Hall and stairs leading to up-stairs bedrooms

Reception area

Visitors signing in—out book

Entrance to the service users/visitors sitting room

Service users/visitors sitting and dinning room

Comfy chairs

Radiator

Dinning tables

Television

Carpet floor

Kitchen area

Office area

This care home has one main door that leads in and out of the building. This door is not locked during the day meaning anyone can gain entry to the building.

There is a reception desk that is manned by a receptionist during the day, however it is not manned during the receptionists breaks or during the night. This is a potential hazard as people may enter the building without the care home being aware.

There is a signing in book for all visitors to complete when they enter the premises, how-ever some visitors forget to sign in or out causing the care home to not be fully aware of how many people are on site at any one time.

The entrance hall into the building also leads to the stairs that take you to the service users bedrooms. This is a potential hazard as visitors can access the clients bedrooms without permission at times when the recep-tion desk is unmanned.

The service users lounge/dinning room is also directly off the hall way. This is for easy access for the visitors to find their family member. However this could be a potential hazard as the dinning room could become over crowded with visitors and clients.

The use of colour and being word processed gives the leaflet a great finish.

The learner has considered the hazards in the care home well, stating where the hazard is and why it is a hazard.

Ask your assessor for a signed observation record confirming that you performed to a satisfactory standard. Some grading criteria can only be met if you do this.

The observation record should state where and when you completed the activity.

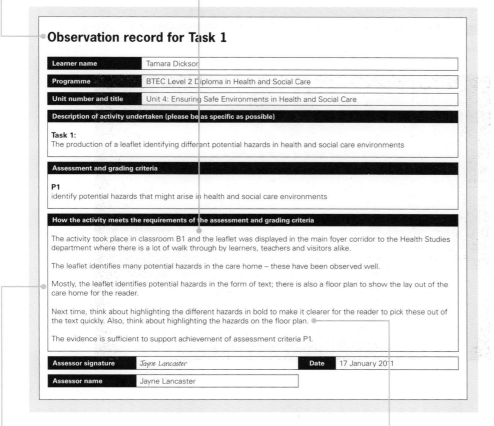

Observation record for Task 1

Learner name	Tamara Dickson
Programme	BTEC Level 2 Diploma in Health and Social Care
Unit number and title	Unit 4: Ensuring Safe Environments in Health and Social Care

Description of activity undertaken (please be as specific as possible)

Task 1:
The production of a leaflet identifying different potential hazards in health and social care environments

Assessment and grading criteria

P1
identify potential hazards that might arise in health and social care environments

How the activity meets the requirements of the assessment and grading criteria

The activity took place in classroom B1 and the leaflet was displayed in the main foyer corridor to the Health Studies department where there is a lot of walk through by learners, teachers and visitors alike.

The leaflet identifies many potential hazards in the care home – these have been observed well.

Mostly, the leaflet identifies potential hazards in the form of text; there is also a floor plan to show the lay out of the care home for the reader.

Next time, think about highlighting the different hazards in bold to make it clearer for the reader to pick these out of the text quickly. Also, think about highlighting the hazards on the floor plan.

The evidence is sufficient to support achievement of assessment criteria P1.

Assessor signature	Jayne Lancaster	**Date**	17 January 2011
Assessor name	Jayne Lancaster		

The assessor should discuss on the observation form what evidence you have produced.

Usually, the assessor will suggest on the observation form what improvements you could make in the future.

The title of the poster is in a large font size so it can be seen from a distance.

This poster contributes to the criteria, but does not meet the criteria alone, as the criteria asks for health and safety legislation (suggesting that there is more than one).

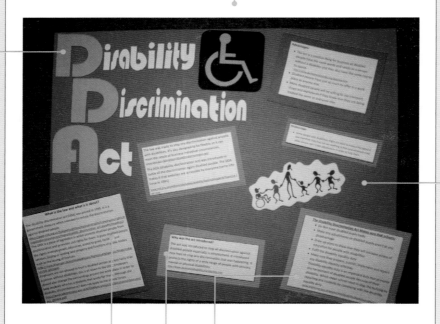

Sample learner work: page 3

Task 2a: Poster to outline a piece of health and safety legislation

The poster has been split into sections, making it more reader friendly.

The poster contains lots of information, but could do with a few pictures to use as examples.

Check that the task activity relates correctly to the activity on your assignment sheet and observation record.

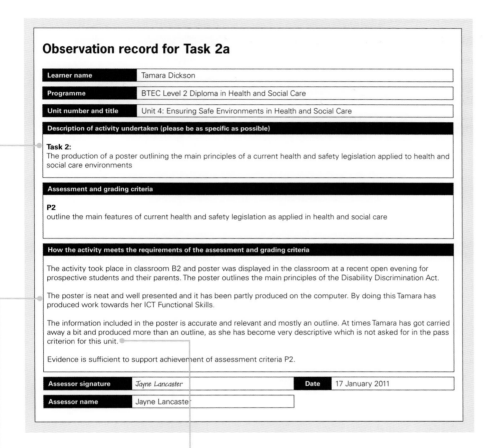

Observation record for Task 2a

Learner name	Tamara Dickson
Programme	BTEC Level 2 Diploma in Health and Social Care
Unit number and title	Unit 4: Ensuring Safe Environments in Health and Social Care

Description of activity undertaken (please be as specific as possible)

Task 2:
The production of a poster outlining the main principles of a current health and safety legislation applied to health and social care environments

Assessment and grading criteria

P2
outline the main features of current health and safety legislation as applied in health and social care

How the activity meets the requirements of the assessment and grading criteria

The activity took place in classroom B2 and poster was displayed in the classroom at a recent open evening for prospective students and their parents. The poster outlines the main principles of the Disability Discrimination Act.

The poster is neat and well presented and it has been partly produced on the computer. By doing this Tamara has produced work towards her ICT Functional Skills.

The information included in the poster is accurate and relevant and mostly an outline. At times Tamara has got carried away a bit and produced more than an outline, as she has become very descriptive which is not asked for in the pass criterion for this unit.

Evidence is sufficient to support achievement of assessment criteria P2.

Assessor signature	*Jayne Lancaster*	Date	17 January 2011
Assessor name	Jayne Lancaster		

The assessor has linked the poster to ICT Functional Skills as well as to the grading criteria in Unit 4.

The observation record shows that the assessor feels that the learner has written more than she needed to, to achieve the criteria.

This table covers the whole of P2 as it looks at a range of legislation, not just one piece of legislation.

The table is not as detailed as the poster as it is only meant to contain an outline of the main features of the legislation, not a description.

Task 2b: Written report: The main features of health and safety legislation

Legislation/regulations	Overview of the legislation	Legislation strengths (what is good about it?)	Legislation weaknesses (what is not so good about it?)
Health and Safety at Work Act 1974	This piece of legislation was introduced to protect the employees from unsafe working practices. It ensures that employers and employees take reasonable care for the health and safety of themselves and other people that come into their place of work.	Helps to reduce injuries and accidents within the work place. Means people will get training and learn skills in safe practices at work, have regular fire safety and manual handling training.	Cost employers a lot of money for training of their staff. May lose some working time when staff are off doing the training.
The Working Time regulations	These regulations ensure that employers do not make their employees work too long hours and have sufficient rest breaks	Helps to make sure that staff are not working too long hours and stops them from being too tired. Also means if staff are not tired they are less likely to make mistakes.	Not all jobs are covered by the rules and there is an opt out scheme which some companies may use to put pressure on their employees to do.
The Disability Discrimination Act 1995	This Act was put in place to ensure that people with disabilities were given the same opportunities as able-bodied people.	Disabled people can join in with everyday activities exactly the same as people without disabilities.	Some companies might not be able to afford adaption's that need to be made to their premises for disabled people.
Mental Health Act 1983	This Act is used to force some people with severe mental health problems to go into hospital for treatment.	It helps people with very bad mental health problems have access to treatment for their illness. It also helps to keep the patient and the general public safe.	Can take a long time through the courts to get someone in hospital under the Act and only a close relative can appeal against someone being detained under the Act.

Some of your friends may have used a larger font size so that their tables extend over several pages; this just wastes paper.

The learner here has outlined the legislations by giving a little overview of each and mentioned one or two strengths and weaknesses.

Sample work: page 5

Legislation/regulations	Overview of the legislation	Legislation strengths (what is good about it?)	Legislation weaknesses (what is not so good about it?)
COSHH Regulations 2002	COSSH regulations are about the types of chemicals that can be used and the way in which chemicals are stored and used in the work place.	It makes sure good practice is followed and protects people from injury and harm from any chemicals that they may have to work with.	Will cost employers money for equipment like locked cupboards for storing chemicals in and will also cost them and take time risk assessing all chemicals that they use.
RIDDOR 1995	RIDDOR is the reporting of Injuries, Diseases, and dangerous Occurrences regulations 1995. This regulation is about how accidents within the workplace must be reported.	Makes employers be aware of any incidents within their workplace.	Can take a lot of time to fill out forms and can also be confusing as to what does and does not need to be reported.
The Human Rights Act	This Act protects people's rights in life and death matters, including how you are treated in your day-to-day life. They help you to be treated fairly, with respect in what you say and do.	Helps people to not be discriminated against because of their belief, race or culture and lets them have their own opinion and live their life how they would like to.	Because there are so many things that this Act can include it can be very difficult to understand.
The Health and Safety (First-Aid) Regulations 1981	This regulation requires employers to provide suitable equipment and facilities to make sure their staff can receive first aid if they are sick or injured while at work.	Applies to all work places regardless of the amount of people that work there.	Some companies may find it hard to afford the cost of training their staff and might cause staff shortages whilst staff are on training courses. Smaller businesses may find it hard to get someone interested in becoming a first aider.
Manual Handling regulations 1992	These regulations ensure employers reduce the risk as much as possible of their staff getting injured or harmed, by any lifting or moving procedures that may be involved within their job.	Makes employers aware of any injuries caused by lifting and moving. Also ensures employers provide correct manual handling training for their staff.	Training can be expensive and can cause staffing problems when employees are away on training

You can work as a group to talk about the different legislation, but the written work must be your own.

Tables are a great way of organising all your information into manageable pieces. It is easy to read and to use later for other assignments.

Assessor's comments

For any assignment, always check that you are achieving the pass (P) criteria. To achieve an overall pass for a unit, you must get all the Ps signed off.

Detailing what you enjoyed and also any problems that you had will help you in future assignments, as you will know what to do differently to avoid similar problems.

You should always read and take note of the assessor's feedback; in this case they have praised the learner. If there had been problems with the evidence then this is where they would give guidance on how to improve and achieve.

Your assessor will write either "Yes" or "No" in this box to let you know if you have achieved the criteria.

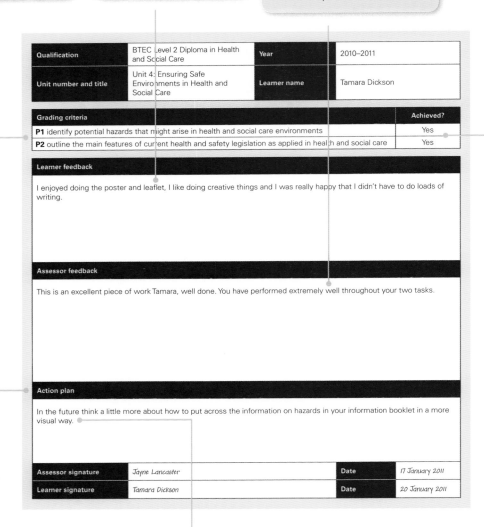

| Qualification | BTEC Level 2 Diploma in Health and Social Care | Year | 2010–2011 |
| Unit number and title | Unit 4: Ensuring Safe Environments in Health and Social Care | Learner name | Tamara Dickson |

Grading criteria			Achieved?
P1 identify potential hazards that might arise in health and social care environments			Yes
P2 outline the main features of current health and safety legislation as applied in health and social care			Yes

Learner feedback

I enjoyed doing the poster and leaflet, I like doing creative things and I was really happy that I didn't have to do loads of writing.

Assessor feedback

This is an excellent piece of work Tamara, well done. You have performed extremely well throughout your two tasks.

Action plan

In the future think a little more about how to put across the information on hazards in your information booklet in a more visual way.

| Assessor signature | Jayne Lancaster | | Date | 17 January 2011 |
| Learner signature | Tamara Dickson | | Date | 20 January 2011 |

No further action is needed because the learner has completed all the tasks to the required standard. If the assessor had identified a problem then the way to resolve it would be outlined here.

Although no further action is needed, the assessor has still commented on things that the learner should consider for future assignments.

Coping with problems

Most learners sail through their BTEC First with no major problems. Unfortunately, not everyone is so lucky. Some may have personal difficulties or other issues that disrupt their work so they are late handing in their assignments. If this happens to you, it's vital to know what to do. This checklist should help.

Checklist for coping with problems

✔ Check that you know who to talk to.

✔ Don't sit on a problem and worry about it. Talk to someone promptly, in confidence. It's always easier to cope if you've shared it with someone.

✔ Most centres have professional counsellors you can talk to if you prefer. They won't repeat anything you say to them without your permission.

✔ If you've done something wrong or silly, people will respect you more if you are honest, admit where you went wrong and apologise promptly.

Case study: Seeking help

Max talks about a problem he experienced on his BTEC First in Health and Social Care course.

'I made a really good start on my course and I was really pleased with the grades I got for the first three assignments I had completed. It was during the second term of my course when things started to go wrong.

I live with my dad and younger brother. My mum had left over the Christmas holidays and my dad was working very hard to provide for us, which meant he couldn't always pick Jimmy up from school. I had to go home early from college quite a few times to look after him and this caused problems with my tutor and friends on the course.

At first I didn't want to tell anyone why I was leaving early. I was still upset about my mum and dad splitting up and didn't want to talk about it. It all came to a head when I missed a presentation I was meant to be

doing. I had to attend a tutorial with my personal tutor and it all just came out. I felt really stupid getting upset in front of him, but he was really great about it. He gave me an extension on my presentation and over the next few weeks we worked out a plan which let me leave early when I had to. He also encouraged me to explain to my dad that there were some sessions I really couldn't miss. Dad listened to me and was able to arrange more flexible hours at work and so we are coping much better now.

If I were to give advice to anyone having problems affecting their work on their course (no matter which course it was), I would tell them to speak to their tutor before things get out of hand. Just talking through the problem can often help and in many cases they may be able to work out a plan to help them through the problems.'

TOP TIPS

If you have a serious complaint or concern, talk to your chosen tutor first – for example if you believe an assignment grade is unfair. All centres have official procedures to cover important issues such as appeals about assignments and formal complaints, but it's sensible to try to resolve a problem informally first.

Activity: Identifying help available

Knowing where to go if you have a problem is really important.

Find out who you would go to discuss the following problems or issues:

Issue or problem	Where would you go for help?
You don't understand why you have been given a low grade for an assignment.	
You are struggling to meet the deadline for a piece of work.	
You need help completing a written piece of work.	
You are having difficulty finding money for travel costs.	
You are having second thoughts about the course you have chosen.	

Skills building

To do your best in your assignments you need a number of skills, including:
- your **personal, learning and thinking skills**
- your **functional skills** of ICT, mathematics and English
- your proofreading and document-production skills.

Personal, learning and thinking skills (PLTS)

These are the skills, personal qualities and behaviour that you find in people who are effective and confident at work. These people enjoy carrying out a wide range of tasks, always try to do their best and work well alone or with others. They enjoy a challenge and use new experiences to learn and develop.

Activity: How good are your PLTS?

1   Do this quiz to help you identify areas for improvement.

    a) I get on well with other people.

        Always   **Usually**   **Seldom**   **Never**

    b) I try to find out other people's suggestions for solving problems that puzzle me.

        Always   **Usually**   **Seldom**   **Never**

    c) I plan carefully to make sure I meet my deadlines.

        Always   **Usually**   **Seldom**   **Never**

    d) If someone is being difficult, I think carefully before making a response.

        Always   **Usually**   **Seldom**   **Never**

    e) I don't mind sharing my possessions or my time.

        Always   **Usually**   **Seldom**   **Never**

    f) I take account of other people's views and opinions.

        Always   **Usually**   **Seldom**   **Never**

    g) I enjoy thinking of new ways of doing things.

        Always   **Usually**   **Seldom**   **Never**

    h) I like creating new and different things.

        Always   **Usually**   **Seldom**   **Never**

    i) I enjoy planning and finding ways of solving problems.

        Always   **Usually**   **Seldom**   **Never**

j) I enjoy getting feedback about my performance.

Always   Usually   Seldom   Never

k) I try to learn from constructive criticism so that I know what to improve.

Always   Usually   Seldom   Never

l) I enjoy new challenges.

Always   Usually   Seldom   Never

m) I am even-tempered.

Always   Usually   Seldom   Never

n) I am happy to make changes when necessary.

Always   Usually   Seldom   Never

o) I like helping other people.

Always   Usually   Seldom   Never

Score 3 points for each time you answered 'Always', 2 points for 'Usually', 1 point for 'Seldom' and 0 points for 'Never'. The higher your score, the higher your personal, learning and thinking skills.

2 How creative are you? Test yourself with this activity. Identify 50 different objects you could fit into a matchbox at the same time! As a start, three suitable items are a postage stamp, a grain of rice, a staple. Can you find 47 more?

Functional skills

Functional skills are the practical skills you need to function confidently, effectively and independently at work, when studying and in everyday life. They focus on the following areas:

- Information and Communications Technology (ICT)
- Maths
- English.

You may already be familiar with functional skills. Your BTEC First tutors will give you more information about how you will continue to develop these skills on your new course.

ICT skills

These will relate directly to how much 'hands-on' practice you have had on IT equipment. You may be an experienced IT user and using word processing, spreadsheet and presentation software may be second nature. Searching for information online may be something you do every day – in between downloading music, buying or selling on eBay and updating your Facebook profile!

BTEC FACTS

Your BTEC First qualification is at Level 2. Qualifications in functional skills start at Entry level and continue to Level 2. (You don't need to achieve functional skills to gain any BTEC qualification and the evidence from a BTEC assignment can't be used towards the assessment of functional skills.)

Or you may prefer to avoid computer contact as much as possible. If so, there are two things you need to do.

1 Use every opportunity to improve your ICT skills so that you can start to live in the 21st century!

2 Make life easier by improving your basic proofreading and document preparation skills.

Proofreading and document preparation skills

Being able to produce well-displayed work quickly will make your life a lot easier. On any course there will be at least one unit that requires you to use good document preparation skills.

Tips to improve your document production skills

✔ If your keyboarding skills are poor, ask if there is a workshop you can join. Or your library or resource centre may have software you can use.

✔ Check that you know the format of documents you have to produce for assignments. It can help to have a 'model' version of each type in your folder for quick reference.

✔ Practise checking your work by reading word by word – and remember not to rely on spellcheckers.

Activity: How good are your ICT skills?

1a)   Test your current ICT abilities by responding *honestly* to each of the following statements.

i) I can create a copy of my timetable using a word-processing or spreadsheet package.
True   **False**

ii) I can devise and design a budget for myself for the next three months using a spreadsheet package.
True   **False**

iii) I can email a friend who has just got broadband to say how to minimise the danger of computer viruses, what a podcast is and also explain the restrictions on music downloads.
True   **False**

iv) I can use presentation software to prepare a presentation containing four or five slides on a topic of my choice.
True   **False**

v) I can research online to compare the performance and prices of laptop computers and prepare an information sheet using word-processing software.
True   **False**

vi) I can prepare a poster, with graphics, for my mother's friend, who is starting her own business preparing children's party food, and attach it to an email to her for approval.
True   **False**

TRY THIS

Learning to touch type can save you hours of time. To check your keyboarding skills go to page 90 to see how to access a useful website.

TOP TIPS

Print your work on good paper and keep it flat so that it looks good when you hand it in.

1b) Select any one of the above to which you answered false and learn how to do it.

2 Compare the two tables below. The first is an original document; the second is a typed copy. Are they identical? Highlight any differences you find and check them with the key on page 89.

Name	Date	Time	Room
Abbott	16 July	9.30 am	214
Grey	10 August	10.15 am	160
Johnston	12 August	2.20 pm	208
Waverley	18 July	3.15 pm	180
Jackson	30 September	11.15 am	209
Gregory	31 August	4.20 pm	320
Marshall	10 September	9.30 am	170
Bradley	16 September	2.20 pm	210

Name	Date	Time	Room
Abbott	26 July	9.30 am	214
Gray	10 August	10.15 am	160
Johnson	12 August	2.20 pm	208
Waverley	18 July	3.15 am	180
Jackson	31 September	11.15 am	209
Gregory	31 August	4.20 pm	320
Marshall	10 September	9.30 pm	170
Bradley	16 August	2.20 pm	201

Maths or numeracy skills

Four easy ways to improve your numeracy skills

1 Work out simple calculations in your head, like adding up the prices of items you are buying. Then check if you are correct when you pay for them.

2 Set yourself numeracy problems based on your everyday life. For example, if you are on a journey that takes 35 minutes and you leave home at 11.10am, what time will you arrive? If you are travelling at 40 miles an hour, how long will it take you to go 10 miles?

3 Treat yourself to a Maths Training program.

4 Go to page 90 to check out online sites to improve your skills.

TOP TIPS

Quickly test answers. For example, if fuel costs 85p a litre and someone is buying 15 litres, estimate this at £1 x 15 (£15) and the answer should be just below this. So if your answer came out at £140, you'd immediately know you'd done something wrong!

Activity: How good are your maths skills?

Answer as many of the following questions as you can in 15 minutes. Check your answers with the key on page 89.

1 a) 12 + 28 = ?

  i) 30　　**ii) 34**　　**iii) 38**　　**iv) 40**　　**v) 48**

  b) 49 ÷ 7 = ?

  i) 6　　**ii) 7**　　**iii) 8**　　**iv) 9**　　**v) 10**

  c) ½ + 1¼ = ?

  i) ¾　　**ii) 1½**　　**iii) 1¾**　　**iv) 2¼**　　**v) 3**

  d) 4 × 12 = 8 × ?

  i) 5　　**ii) 6**　　**iii) 7**　　**iv) 8**　　**v) 9**

  e) 16.5 + 25.25 − ? = 13.25

  i) 28.5　　**ii) 31.25**　　**iii) 34.5**　　**iv) 41.65**　　**v) 44**

2 a) You buy four items at £1.99, two at 98p and three at £1.75. You hand over a £20 note. How much change will you get? _____

  b) What fraction of one litre is 250 ml? _____

  c) What percentage of £50 is £2.50? _____

  d) A designer travelling on business can claim 38.2p a mile in expenses. How much is she owed if she travels 625 miles? _____

  e) You are flying to New York in December. New York is five hours behind British time and the flight lasts eight hours. If you leave at 11.15 am, what time will you arrive? _____

  f) For your trip to the United States you need American dollars. You find that the exchange rate is $1.5 dollars.

  i) How many dollars will you receive if you exchange £500? _____

  ii) Last year your friend visited New York when the exchange rate was $1.8. She also exchanged £500. Did she receive more dollars than you or fewer – and by how much? _____

  g) A security guard and his dog patrol the perimeter fence of a warehouse each evening. The building is 480 metres long and 300 metres wide and the fence is 80 metres out from the building on all sides. If the guard and his dog patrol the fence three times a night, how far will they walk? _____

English skills

Your English skills affect your ability to understand what you read, prepare a written document, say what you mean and understand other people. Even if you're doing a practical subject, there will always be times when you need to leave someone a note, tell them about a phone call, read or listen to instructions – or write a letter for a job application!

Six easy ways to improve your English skills

1 Read more. It increases the number of words you know and helps to make you familiar with correct spellings.

2 Look up words you don't understand in a dictionary and check their meaning. Then try to use them yourself to increase your vocabulary.

3 Do crosswords. These help increase your vocabulary and practise your spelling at the same time.

4 You can use websites to help you get to grips with English vocabulary, grammar and punctuation. Go to page 90 to see how to access relevant websites.

5 Welcome opportunities to practise speaking in class, in discussion groups and during presentations – rather than avoiding them!

6 Test your ability to listen to someone else by seeing how much you can remember when they've finished speaking.

Activity: How good are your English skills?

1 In the table below are 'wrong' versions of words often spelled incorrectly. Write the correct spellings on the right. Check your list against the answers on page 89.

Incorrect spelling	Correct spelling
accomodation	
seperate	
definate	
payed	
desparate	
acceptible	
competant	
succesful	

2 Correct the error(s) in these sentences.

    a) The plug on the computer is lose.

    b) The car was stationery outside the house.

    c) Their going on they're holidays tomorrow.

    d) The principle of the college is John Smith.

    e) We are all going accept Tom.

3 Punctuate these sentences correctly.

    a) Toms train was late on Monday and Tuesday.

    b) She is going to France Belgium Spain and Italy in the summer.

    c) He comes from Leeds and says its great there.

4 Read the article on copyright.

Copyright

Anyone who uses a photocopier can break copyright law if they carry out unrestricted photocopying of certain documents. This is because The Copyright, Designs and Patents Act 1988 protects the creator of an original work against having it copied without permission.

Legally, every time anyone writes a book, composes a song, makes a film or creates any other type of artistic work, this work is treated as their property (or copyright). If anyone else wishes to make use of it, they must get permission to do so and, on occasions, pay a fee.

Licences can be obtained to allow educational establishments to photocopy limited numbers of some publications. In addition, copies of an original document can be made for certain specific purposes. These include research and private study. Under the Act, too, if an article is summarised and quoted by anyone, then the author and title of the original work must be acknowledged.

a) Test your ability to understand unfamiliar information by responding to the following statements with 'True' or 'False'.

 i) Students and tutors in schools and colleges can copy anything they want.
  True False

 ii) The law which covers copyright is The Copyright, Designs and Patents Act 1988.
  True False

 iii) A student photocopying a document in the library must have a licence.
  True False

 iv) Copyright only relates to books in the library.
  True False

 v) If you quote a newspaper report in an assignment, you don't need to state the source.
  True False

 vii) Anyone is allowed to photocopy a page of a book for research purposes.
  True False

b) Make a list of key points in the article, then write a brief summary in your own words.

5 Nikki has read a newspaper report that a horse racing in the Kentucky Derby had to be put down. The filly collapsed and the vet couldn't save her. Nikki says it's the third time in two years a racehorse has had to be put down in the US. As a horse lover she is convinced racing should be banned in Britain and the US. She argues that fox hunting was banned to protect foxes, and that racehorses are more important and more expensive than foxes. Darren disagrees. He says the law is not working, hardly anyone has been prosecuted and fox hunting is going on just like before. Debbie says that animals aren't important whilst there is famine in the world.

a) Do you think the three arguments are logical? See if you can spot the flaws and check your ideas with the suggestions on page 89.

b) Sporting activities and support for sporting teams often provoke strong opinions. For a sport or team of your choice, identify two opposing views that might be held. Then decide how you would give a balanced view. Test your ideas with a friend or family member.

Answers

Skills building answers

ICT activities

2 Differences between the two tables are highlighted in bold.

Name	Date	Time	Room
Abbott	**16** July	9.30 am	214
Grey	10 August	10.15 am	160
Johnston	12 August	2.20 pm	208
Waverley	18 July	3.15 **pm**	180
Jackson	**30** September	11.15 am	209
Gregory	31 August	4.20 pm	320
Marshall	10 September	9.30 **am**	170
Bradley	16 **September**	2.20 pm	**210**

Maths/numeracy activities

1 a) iv, **b)** ii, **c)** iii, **d)** ii, **e)** i

2 a) £4.83, **b)** ¼, **c)** 5%, **d)** £238.75, **e)** 2.15 pm, **f) i)** $750 **ii)** $150 dollars more, **g)** 6.6 km.

English activities

1 Spellings: accommodation, separate, definite, paid, desperate, acceptable, competent, successful

2 Errors:
   a) The plug on the computer is <u>loose</u>.
   b) The car was <u>stationary</u> outside the house.
   c) <u>They're</u> going on <u>their</u> holidays tomorrow.
   d) The <u>principal</u> of the college is John Smith.
   e) We are all going <u>except</u> Tom.

3 Punctuation:
   a) Tom's train was late on Monday and Tuesday.
   b) She is going to France, Belgium, Spain and Italy in the summer.
   c) He comes from Leeds and says it's great there.

4 a) i) False, **ii)** True, **iii)** False, **iv)** False, **v)** False, **vi)** False, **vii)** True

5 A logical argument would be that if racehorses are frequently injured in a particular race, eg one with difficult jumps, then it should not be held. It is not logical to compare racehorses with foxes. The value of the animal is irrelevant if you are assessing cruelty. Darren's argument is entirely different and unrelated to Nikki's. Whether or not fox hunting legislation is effective or not has no bearing on the danger (or otherwise) to racehorses. Finally, famine is a separate issue altogether. You cannot logically 'rank' problems in the world to find a top one and ignore the others until this is solved!

Subject-specific answers

Quiz

Page 62

How did you do?

Mostly 'a's - You like to keep your head down and avoid difficult issues. This might be because you don't like to get into difficult situations, but it will not be helpful when preparing, delivering or even watching presentations.

Mostly 'b's – You are generally well organised and supportive of others. You should do well.

Mostly 'c's – Although there are times when being firm with people is important you should always try to be fair. You will get more from your work if you try to be more supportive of others.

Command words wordsearch

Page 67

a) contrast
b) explain
c) analyse
d) justify
e) outline
f) compare
g) state
h) identify
i) describe
j) evaluate

E	S	Y	L	A	N	A	X	I	E
V	I	Y	F	I	T	S	U	J	R
A	N	F	L	I	A	E	A	C	A
L	I	S	O	S	T	T	O	L	P
U	A	A	E	U	S	N	R	E	M
A	L	U	R	J	T	U	E	J	O
T	P	J	S	R	O	L	C	D	C
E	X	A	A	A	M	V	I	O	I
D	E	S	C	R	I	B	E	N	D
D	T	R	T	E	S	T	A	T	E

Accessing website links

Links to various websites are referred to throughout this BTEC Level 2 First Study Skills Guide. In order to ensure that these links are up-to-date, that they work and that the sites aren't inadvertently linked to any material that could be considered offensive, we have made the links available on our website: www.pearsonhotlinks.co.uk. When you visit the site, please enter the title BTEC Level 2 First in Health and Social Care, or the ISBN 9781846905742 to gain access to the website links and information on how they can be used to help you with your studies.

Useful terms

Apprenticeships
Schemes that enable you to work and earn money at the same time as you gain further qualifications (an NVQ award and a technical certificate) and improve your functional skills. Apprentices learn work-based skills relevant to their job role and their chosen industry. See page 90 for information about how to access a link where you can find out more.

Assessment methods
Methods, such as practical tasks and assignments, which are used to check that your work demonstrates the learning and understanding you need to obtain the qualification.

Assessor
The tutor who marks or assesses your work.

Assignment
A complete task or mini-**project** set to meet specific grading criteria.

Assignment brief
The information and instructions related to a particular assignment.

BTEC Level 3 Nationals
Qualifications you can take when you have successfully achieved a Level 2 qualification, such as BTEC First. They are offered in a variety of subjects.

Credit value
The number of credits attached to your BTEC course. The credit value increases relative to the length of time you need to complete the course, from 15 credits for a BTEC Certificate, to 30 credits for a BTEC Extended Certificate and 60 credits for a BTEC Diploma.

Command word
The word in an assignment that tells you what you have to do to produce the type of answer that is required, eg 'list', 'describe', 'analyse'.

Educational Maintenance Award (EMA)
This is a means-tested award which provides eligible learners under 19, who are studying a full-time course at a centre, with a cash sum of money every week. See page 90 for information about how to access a link where you can find out more.

Functional skills
The practical skills that enable all learners to use and apply English, Maths and ICT both at work and in their everyday lives. They aren't compulsory to achieve on the course, but are of great use to you.

Grade
The rating of pass, merit or distinction that is given to an assignment you have completed, which identifies the standard you have achieved.

Grading criteria
The standard you have to demonstrate to obtain a particular grade in the unit. In other words, what you have to prove you can do.

Grading grid
The table in each unit of your BTEC qualification specification that sets out the grading criteria.

Indicative reading
Recommended books, magazines, journals and websites whose content is both suitable and relevant to the unit.

Induction
A short programme of events at the start of a course or work placement designed to give you essential information and introduce you to other people so that you can settle in easily.

Internal verification
The quality checks carried out by nominated tutors at all centres to ensure that all assignments are at the right level and cover appropriate learning outcomes. The checks also ensure that all **assessors** are marking work consistently and to the same standards.

Learning outcomes
The learning and skills you must demonstrate to show that you have learned a unit effectively.

Levels of study

The depth, breadth and complexity of knowledge, understanding and skills required to achieve a qualification determines its level. Level 2 is equivalent to GCSE level (grades A* to C). Level 3 equates to GCE A-level. As you successfully achieve one level, you can progress on to the next. BTEC qualifications are offered at Entry Level, then Levels 1, 2, 3, 4, 5, 6 and 7.

Mandatory units

On a BTEC Level 2 First course, these are the compulsory units that all learners must complete to gain the qualification.

Optional units

Units on your course from which you may be able to make a choice. They help you specialise your skills, knowledge and understanding and may help progression into work or further education.

Personal, learning and thinking skills (PLTS)

The skills and qualities that improve your ability to work independently and be more effective and confident at work. Opportunities for developing these are a feature of all BTEC First courses. They aren't compulsory to achieve on the course, but are of great use to you.

Plagiarism

Copying someone else's work or work from any other sources (eg the internet) and passing it off as your own. It is strictly forbidden on all courses.

Portfolio

A collection of work compiled by a learner – for an **assessor** – usually as evidence of learning.

Project

A comprehensive piece of work which normally involves original research and planning and investigation either by an individual or a team. The outcome will vary depending upon the type of project undertaken. For example, it may result in the organisation of a specific event, a demonstration of a skill, a presentation or a piece of writing.

Tutorial

An individual or small group meeting with your tutor at which you discuss the work you are currently doing and other more general course issues.

Unit content

Details about the topics covered by the unit and the knowledge and skills you need to complete it.

Work placement

Time spent on an employer's premises when you carry out work-based tasks as an employee and also learn about the enterprise to develop your skills and knowledge.

Work-related qualification

A qualification designed to help you to develop the knowledge and understanding you need for a particular area of work.